Ka-Ching!

D1310812

Pitt Poetry Series
Ed Ochester, Editor

Ka-Ching!

Denise Duhamel

UNIVERSITY OF PITTSBURGH PRESS

Published by the University of Pittsburgh Press, Pittsburgh, Pa., 15260

Copyright © 2009, Denise Duhamel

All rights reserved

Manufactured in the United States of America

Printed on acid-free paper

10 9 8 7 6 5 4 3 2

ISBN 13: 978-0-8229-6021-8

ISBN 10: 0-8229-6021-4

for Janet Duhamel and in memory of Normand Duhamel (1927–2008)

Contents

one-armed bandits

big tip

play money

$100,000

As a kid I loved being the banker in Monopoly, in The Game of Life—the pink and yellow bills not quite as big as our U.S. currency, but closer to food stamps. The board games had no coins, snubbing the paltry dimes of hobos and kids. I had a penny collection, round slots in a blue cardboard folder, and I'd search for dates while rummaging through my parents' change, hunting for pennies that became worth more than pennies, the value of what is rare. The 1943 copper alloy penny, the 1955 penny with the year stamped twice, the 1924 penny with the letter "S" after the date. I loved rolling coins in wrappers, my favorite being the quarters with their hefty ten-dollar payoff; my least favorite the nickels, the same amount of trouble for only two dollars, even though I kept a lookout for one of those rare 1913–1938 buffalos. My grandmother gave me a porcelain bank, not a piggy but a cat, and I filled it within a year, not realizing there was no hole with a rubber stopper on the bottom, no way to get the money out. There are still coins in the bottom of that cat! I tried my best to slip them out with a knife through the slot in the kitty's head, but even after several days at the kitchen table, I couldn't retrieve a few fifty-cent pieces, though I remembered their clinkety-clanks going in. There is a metaphor here somewhere, that making money can be messy and aggressive, that wimps like me will never truly take a hammer to a gift. I was a teenager by the time the bicentennial quarters went into circulation, a Revolutionary drummer on the back instead of an eagle. They were too plentiful to warrant collecting—or maybe I was just too busy working as a supermarket cashier after school, making sure all the heads on my bills were facing the same way. I'd open a roll of coins by banging them on the tray in my drawer without a thought to the children's ghost fingers stacking them, learning to count. Now I'm too busy to roll. I recently dumped a plastic bag full of change in a coin changer, and even after the machine's commission, got seventy dollars. I am richer than I ever imagined I'd be. I've held lira, pesetas, pounds, and now the Euro—peach, aqua, embellished with silver stripes. As a teenager I loved being the banker in Monopoly, in The Game of Life, the pink and yellow bills vaguely what I thought of as sophisticated, European.

3

$200,000

When my father's father died, my parents used the money from the inheritance and took my sister and me on a cruise. They blew the whole thing—what the heck—my family had never been on a real vacation before. My grandfather was a renter all his life and lived in a cold-water flat with my grandmother, who had passed away just a few years earlier. I got my first real sunburn on that cruise, the deliciously cold scratchy sheets of the cabin bed against my shoulders. There were candies on our pillows each night, and towels folded into bird shapes. Apparently, my grandfather didn't trust banks and had stuffed money under his mattress. My sister's bathing suit was yellow and mine was blue plaid. My father and his two brothers divvied up the cash as though the currency were a deck of cards. At kiddie bingo, my sister won a sailor doll and I, ten play money bills, each labeled $100,000. My mother looked like a glamorous As the World Turns actress in her white cocktail dress and gold sling backs. One night a waiter brought a cake for her birthday and kissed her on the cheek. My parents sipped neon-colored drinks at the bar. My mother kept saying that she was a lady of leisure that week, that she could certainly get used to this. I was getting used to it, too—my cool million with Woodrow Wilson's face on each bill. I was careful not to crumple the oversized dollars as I carried them in my straw bag with the seashells glued to the front. I played Marco Polo with some kids whose father, a banker from Denver, told me that $100,000 was the largest banknote ever made. I was really impressed until he explained that, even if my play money suddenly turned real, I couldn't spend it because the bills could only be used for government transactions. My dad was obsessed with a busty woman who wore a glittery silver bikini—my mom was too, so they took her picture from the deck above. She's in our scrapbook, sharing the pages with my grandparents. We missed them—they were with us as we splashed in the pool, as we crawled along in the glass-bottomed boat, on our excursion in Nassau. The local boys crowded us when we first got off the cruise ship, their hands out, asking for coins. My sister and I were afraid. But our father, along with the other men, started throwing nickels and quarters into the water and the boys happily dove in to get them.

$300,000

According to a survey in a women's magazine, women are more comfortable discussing their weight than their savings account balances. The trouble with divulging a woman's monetary worth is this: if she's accrued a hefty amount, she's afraid her friends will get jealous or expect her to constantly pick up the tab; if she has a low balance, she'll feel like a loser. And we all know the only good loss is weight loss. It's bad to lose track of your carbohydrates, lose sleep over what you ate or what you spent, lose sight of the big picture, lose the thread of the story, lose touch with reality, lose your temper, lose headway, lose heart, lose hope, lose control, lose it. One night I lost the leather jacket my husband gave me. I left it in the Angelika, an overpriced movie theater with tiny screens that we loved regardless. We were walking toward the Old Town Bar, which was featured in *Boiler Room*, making us crave the burgers there. We were animated, discussing the film, when I felt a chill. I ran back to the theater before the next showing, straight to the seat I'd just left. I checked under the chairs of each and every row, asked strangers if they'd found a jacket. I finally had to give up as the coming attractions began. Any of the characters in the movie would have taken my jacket if they'd found it, but maybe an honest person had brought it to the concession stand? To the manager's office? I was panicky, snuffling, waiting for a lecture. My husband said, *It's OK. It's only a coat.* He was still up for burgers, and I was glad, thinking perhaps that our date was ruined. We popped into the Astor Place Kmart where I bought an "I ♥ New York" sweatshirt, my stab at self-castigation. We agreed our favorite scene in the film was the one in which the young brokers sit around watching a DVD of *Wall Street*, reciting Michael Douglas's and Charlie Sheen's lines from memory. While the characters in *Boiler Room* were nostalgic for the eighties, Nick and I were nostalgic for the even earlier days of bankbooks, the passport-like pages onto which an actual teller would write in your deposits and withdrawals. They were tangible, like our fat burgers at Old Town. I peeled off the bun and pushed aside my fries. I'd finally achieved my goal and didn't want to mess up—at last I weighed less than the number of dollars in my savings account. I'd worked hard. I'm not, by nature, too rich or too thin.

$400,000

My uncle was a big muckety-muck in a supermarket chain. He liked throwing lavish get-togethers with all the complimentary liquor he'd received from buyers. He was the first to serve Pringles, Orville Redenbacher's Gourmet Popcorn, Mrs. Field's Cookies, Starburst Fruit Chews, Reese's Pieces, and Miller Lite—all free samples, he explained. He started voting Republican when he got rich, which led to all kinds of fiery arguments at the Christmas parties he'd host. My uncle had a silver tree decorated with blue glass balls, which seemed the height of luxury to me and a snub to our traditional green one, our folksy homemade ornaments. But even though he drove a Cadillac now, he was loyal to his family, getting his nieces and nephews union jobs at the market as soon as we were sixteen. My high school friends who worked at factories and gas stations marveled at my cushy situation, my yearly raises, the time card I punched—even if I worked only eight minutes extra, the supermarket had to pay me for a full quarter of an hour. I was required to wear a horrid red smock and chirp, *Have a nice day*, the company's slogan, at the end of each transaction. The break room was filthy and the manager a letch. But even so, I knew I had it pretty good. My uncle looked a little like Richard Nixon, whom he defended until the end—*Everyone will remember China, not Watergate*, he said. My uncle's other idol was Frank Perdue with whom he'd had a breakfast meeting once in a Dunkin' Donuts in Boston. He told this story over and over, as though Frank Perdue were as talented as Frank Sinatra. *A hell of a man*, my uncle cooed. *A visionary!* Frank wanted more room for his chickens in the meat case, more Perdue signs. He insisted that the supermarket brand "price comparison" posters be removed. My uncle was Nixon, and Perdue was China. Or maybe it was the other way around. The negotiations were fierce and went on for hours, the waitresses refilling their coffee cups actually changing shifts. My uncle and Frank were on diets but, needing more energy to persevere, decided to split a maple-frosted with sprinkles. When the check came, my uncle tried to pick it up. *No*, Frank said. *I don't want any special favors. Let's go Dutch.* The bill came to $1.33 and Frank Perdue—this is why he was rich, my uncle alleged—debated who should leave that extra penny.

$500,000

When I was in first grade, I discovered a set of custom pencils in my Christmas stocking. They were the most beautiful gift I'd ever received, all the pencils red, not yellow, with my full name running in gold block letters down the side. I never used them because I had the bad habit of chewing on my no. 2s, and I thought these monogrammed ones were too expensive to wreck with teeth marks. I just couldn't bring myself to twirl one into my pencil sharpener, which would, in turn, churn out curled shavings that looked like apple peels falling into the trash. When would I ever get such a present again? When I went off to college, my parents gave me a Cross pen, this time my name in silver cursive. I kept it in its box, sure I would lose it to a library cubicle or to the bottom of my backpack. *I'll use it when I get my first real job*, I told myself. I used the same compact of blush from 1979–2002, when the brush finally fell apart. I'd bought the blush for my high school prom. Because of my allergies, I never wore much makeup, which seemed like such a waste of money anyway, but even I had to admit twenty-three years was a long time to hold onto one compact. I reluctantly purchased another one—Clinique—the day my friend Melissa was having her art opening. Melissa was obsessed with Anne Frank and—because Anne had been interested in sewing—made several dresses with labels stitched into them that read "made by Anne Frank." On a table was a scattering of pencils just like I'd received in my stocking, with Anne Frank's name on them instead. The pencils were an eerie symbol of what she would never get to write. Gallery-goers were asked to take them, as Melissa wanted people to continue Anne's story. *Where did you get these?* I asked Melissa. I wondered how she could afford to give them away. *That's where I got the labels, too. The pencils were really cheap! Maybe fifteen cents each.* Melissa's show was a big success—its simplicity, its ethereal impact. The blush, then the pencils led me to search for the Cross pen, since I'd been working fulltime now for over a decade. I had an idea to write about my grandmother, who reused teabags and paper towels, who died having never worn the "good coat" she'd bought years before. Why was she saving that houndstooth check? I twisted open my Cross pen, but the ink had dried up.

$600,000

In 1986, my roommate talked me into getting my first ATM card. We both had checking accounts at Citibank, which became known as Shitibank because it wouldn't divest its South African assets. I stood in a long line with other New Yorkers—but when it was my turn, the sun shone on the screen so I couldn't quite see it. I squinted, took off my sunglasses, then put them back on. My PIN didn't work—maybe I was doing something wrong? I tried my code again, along with several variations, until the machine swallowed my card. For one of her gallery shows, Sophie Calle photographed people through the security cameras at Paris ATMs. The baffled, the frustrated, the blasé, the elated dad with his toddler on his shoulders. I was inspired to do a spin-off project about PIN numbers—not simple birthday codes, but the codes of obsessions: bingo2, leather88, Whitman13. Of course, my project stayed preconceptual. Who would tell me their passwords? Even if I convinced them that I was an honest person, that more than one time in the early days of ATMs, I'd walked up to a machine that read *Can I help you with anything else?* because a customer had left too soon. A few times I pressed *yes*, but only to check a stranger's checking account balance—I never attempted to withdraw even twenty dollars. At some point, my roommate started being late with her rent, which terrified me, as my name was the only name on the lease. She started borrowing my sweaters and stuffing them, smelling like smoke, back in my drawer. She'd come into my room in the middle of the night, crying about the abortion—she still owed me for that, too. She'd lost her job as a receptionist because two lines rang at once, and she just shut off the ringer. When she was three months behind, I told her she'd have to leave. She said I'd go far in this world because I was a conscienceless bitch, even though I'd changed from Shitibank to Chemical. When she moved out, she took everything we'd bought together—ice cube trays, the shower curtain, a throw rug, a teakettle. When I mopped her empty room, I found a red mesh bag filled with candy coins covered in gold foil—the chocolate was cheap, a bit waxy, but the foil was sturdy—and when I was careful enough, I could pull off one of the serrated paper sides without ripping it and hold what looked like a gold bottle cap in my palm.

$700,000

I was sure I had the job—the interviewers were nodding, smiling, laughing when I attempted a joke. *What are you working on next?* they wanted to know. They thought I showed promise. *Do you think you'd like living in Ohio? Please take a look at these real estate brochures.* I would soon be living in houses like theirs. I'd have a yard and a garden. I'd be hosting parties or buying wine and dessert to bring to their parties. I'd have my own office, maybe a window and a computer and a business card. (I had resisted going to the MLA conference, a meat market for fresh English PhDs who were stiff in their new or borrowed suits, vying like dreary Miss Americas for tenure track lines. The judges were the gray-haired full professors, crinkled, withered—five o'clock shadows on the men, orthopedic shoes on the women. They yawned through candidate presentations and had long lunches paid for by their institutions. But I really wanted this job and going to MLA showed I was serious.) *Perhaps you'd like to start a literary magazine,* they said. *Or run a reading series? Yes yes yes* was my answer to everything. I ran my hands along my lap, along the skirt that I feared I'd only wear once in my life—for this interview—but now I pictured it hanging on a rack with other skirts and blazers, plastic dry cleaner bags over everything, because now I would be able to afford dry cleaning. Underneath, on my closet floor: a row of pumps and a pair of expensive boots on boot trees. I had been on unemployment for four months. Nick was adjuncting, teaching comp. We hadn't been to a dentist or a doctor in years, no insurance. *Oh, just one more thing,* one of the interviewers said as I got up, as I was about to shake all their hands—*How would you teach formal poetry? Sonnets and such.* Easy. I had my answer rehearsed. I cited an anthology by a contemporary who had collected sestinas and pantoums by living poets. I'd used it in a class at my last job, and the students loved it since they could relate to the subject matter. I even used the word groundbreaking to describe it. *OK then,* the chair said. *You'll be hearing from us in a few weeks.* And as I left the hotel suite, I saw the editor of the anthology I'd just praised, sitting in the same chair I'd sat in forty-five minutes earlier. She smoothed her own skirt. I hadn't even reached the elevator when I heard the professors' chiming voices. *Please. Come in.*

9

$800,000

When the Japanese invaded the Philippines, Nick's parents had to flee, pushing a grocery cart containing their silver and their dog Pee Wee through the streets. They reached a cement building, which they heard was out of harm's way. They both were allowed in, though the guard said *Sorry, no dogs* and threw Pee Wee over a fence. Nick's mother cried and would have gladly given her silver tea set or spoons in return for her pet's admission. She only calmed down after meeting a woman whose son had just been killed. Nick's parents were fed canned goods, though their stomachs were jumpy at the sound of the bombs. In pictures, Pee Wee looks like Anna Nicole Smith's dog, Sugar Pie. Anna Nicole who lost her son Daniel at twenty, a few days after giving birth to a baby girl. Anna, so-easy-to-make-fun-of-Anna, fat-Anna, dieting-Anna, sexy-Guess-jeans-model-Anna, marry-an-old-billionaire-Anna, pickle-eating-Anna, Anna-with-her-cousin-with-the-missing-teeth, Supreme-Court-Playboy-Playmate-Anna, Momma Anna. Once I saw a hooker in the meat district who looked exactly like Madonna, or rather exactly like Madonna starring in a movie about a down-and-out hooker, which made me ponder—and not for the first time—who gets rich and who escapes harm. After 9/11, a friend, an Anna Nicole fan, admitted he bought duct tape and plastic, even though the government's plan was soon the butt of jokes on late-night television. Another friend's uncle blew himself up in his own bomb shelter trying to cook a trial meal with propane. But who doesn't have fears? Who doesn't try to prepare for the worst? Remember how, in Margaret Atwood's *A Handmaid's Tale*, women who go to ATMs get a message that their money has been moved into an account of their closest male relative? I have dreamed about that ATM screen many times. So much can go wrong, even when you believe in nest eggs. In one episode of Anna Nicole's reality show, her son ordered a pizza. He seemed like a shy kid, reluctant about cameras. But the obituaries say he was very outgoing, supportive of his mother in all her stages, whether she was a pinup or a mockery of one. When it was safe for Nick's parents to go back home, they walked through the bombed streets and smashed glass. And whom should they meet? Little Pee Wee, loping toward them, wagging his tail.

$900,000

I moved to the Lower East Side in the mid-eighties, the real estate bubble gurgling with greed. My one-bedroom apartment was $900 a month. I had a series of roommates to come up with the rent. I slept in the living room, worked several part-time jobs, and was just starting to pay off my student loans. An old man named Felix had occupied the apartment before me, before he was evicted. He was homeless now and slept near Con Ed because it was warmest there. I'd bring him his Social Security checks, which was the least I could do, since he needed an address to be able to receive them. When I could afford it, I bought him roasted chickens. He said his family was in California and hated him, though I never got the details. This probably had something to do with his love of vodka. He was always holding a bottle, pink spider veins bursting on his nose. The last time I saw him he said he was sorry he was such a bad dad, as though he was confused, as though he thought I was his daughter. Soon after I came home to a bouquet in front of my door—white and yellow carnations for "the family of Felix Strange." I went to Con Ed where Pearl, the homeless woman he'd befriended, told me Felix had died in his sleep. His orange blanket was in her pile now. Then the sympathy cards started to arrive—*in this time of sorrow, thinking of you.* I took the flowers and cards to Pearl. When his next Social Security check came, I called to explain Felix had passed away. A curt woman took down my name and mailed me forms to fill out on his behalf. That's when I saw what he had been paying in rent—$150 a month. I knew there were New York laws about only raising rent a certain percentage from one occupant to the next. I called the housing authority and made a complaint, filling out another questionnaire. I didn't have high expectations that anything would happen, but a few years later my landlord called. Apparently my filing these documents had put a lien on the building, and he wanted to sell. He reduced my rent in half and gave me a refund for the years I'd paid too much. I called Wachovia Bank where the woman who answered assumed I was requesting another deferment on my student loan. No, I said, *I need to find out exactly what I owe since I want to pay the whole thing off.* She put me on speakerphone, so I could hear the whole office cheer.

$1,000,000

After my parents' nearly fatal accident, I thought the one upside would be that they'd sue and become millionaires. They'd travel the world on a cruise, even if it meant that my mother was in a wheelchair now and my father needed extra heart medicine. They'd buy a cushy Cadillac and enjoy a sleek, comfortable ride each time they needed to stock up at the supermarket. *All I want is a new stove,* my mom said. *And maybe a fridge with an icemaker.* She knew not to dream big when it came to the legal system, my sister getting scarcely the price of a new Toyota after suffering a coma as a result of being hit by a drunk driver. But this was different, I thought—the drama of it all, the freakish horror. I took pictures of my mother's scalp, the stitches and swollen hills, sure to convince any jury with a heart. We saved their bloody clothes in a trash bag in the garage, as instructed by the lawyer. As they recovered, my parents spent most of their waking hours on the phone with the hospital's financial office, with Blue Cross. They kept a file cabinet full of claims and statements. Their friends kept egging them on—*Don't accept the first offer. Those insurance companies have deep pockets.* In the meantime, a friend's mother was killed as a result of a hit-and-run. He barely got enough money to pay off her debts. His lawyer told him it's better, financially speaking, if such atrocities happen to young people—*We can't argue that your ninety-year-old mother lost out on any potential earnings, can we?* People seemed to like to quote the case about the McDonald's customer who was burned by hot coffee and sued for 2.9 million dollars. *Surely your parents deserve at least that!* But my father Googled the case, and the woman never got that money. After McDonald's appealed the jury's decision, the woman finally settled out of court. After two years, my parents' lawyer said, *I'm truly sorry—this is the best we can do.* He quoted them a number, which covered their medical expenses, and left almost enough over for a Toyota. *Unless you want to take this to trial—but I have to warn you, that could take up to five years.* My dad was about to turn eighty. My parents live in Rhode Island. The courthouse was in Camden. My father got a new La-Z-Boy, and my mother her fridge. They enjoy iced tea on the porch, perusing travel guides—flipping through Sicily, Hong Kong, Greece.

eBay sonnets

Bidding Time left:
14 minutes

History:
7 bids

The first time I moved to a warm climate
I only lasted four months, fated
to buy back the winter coat I'd donated
to the Combat Zone's Goodwill. I was upset
no one had snagged my coat in my absence.
Was my taste so bad that even the poor
clicked hangers right past my leopard fake fur?
I'd failed in Arizona, now the dense
Boston slush seeped into my plastic boots.
I'd junked a used Corvette in Tucson,
a car that could have been worth a fortune
if I'd only cared to fix it up. Loot
was not yet my forte. I overpaid.
I even got looks of pity from rough trade.

Pity my rough drafts, my false starts, my trade-
mark pink SASE's I was sure would catch
a big editor's attention. But batch
after batch of my poems came back with staid
"no thanks" notes in my inane envelopes.
I worked at Ahab's Rare Books in Cambridge,
selling first editions and unabridged
collections of Alexander Pope,
which made me think longevity was creepy—
some poets relegated to bargain bins
while other poets were like mannequins,
modeling their in-vogue verse obliquely
from their famous graves. I was twenty-one,
I worshipped every poet's skeleton.

Now I bid on each poet's skeleton—
Plath's metacarpus, Sexton's mandible,
Dylan Thomas's expandable
temporal ridge. My screen name is "No-Pun-
Intended," but my eBay friends call me
"No-Pun" for short. I once resold Sappho's
pristine pelvic girdle for a mind-blow-
ing six times what I paid for it. Pretty
good for someone brand new to PayPal.
I still look for book bargains on half.com
but I think the market's future's in bones—
no water damage or fading. Apples
and oranges, some might say: bones and books.
But are they so sure? Have they really looked?

Sure I was fine, I never really looked
at my IRA accounts until
retirement anxiety, middle-
aged angst, set in. I cautiously took
out the folder with my sealed statements
and opened each one, the funds dwindling down
as the dates got closer. I was a clown
with a face full of whipped-cream pie. Fate went
on as I wrote my poems. Contributors'
copies stacked up like confederate bills.
My journals were literary roadkill,
un-auctionable. Financial advisors
say this is common: twenty-somethings blink,
they're forty, then eighty. Life's highest jinks.

In 1984, I might have jinxed
myself for good. My uncle said video
rentals were the next big thing. He owned
a storefront and wanted me to lease *Pink
Panther* tapes to the next generation
of moviegoers who'd watch in the dark
of their living rooms. I was sure this spark

would never catch. Clearly our nation
was built on overpriced popcorn and Cokes,
date nights and bargain matinees, wasn't it?
My uncle proposed a fifty-fifty split,
but I thought the VCR was a joke.
Of course, I always obeyed the sign:
Before Returning, Don't Forget to Rewind.

Next time I return to eBay, I wind
up in the poets' used clothing section—
Marianne Moore's hat, Emily Dickinson's
flannel skirt and gray boots, a real find.
My accountant says I can deduct them
since I wear the clothes while writing poems
I now sell exclusively online. My tomes
on *American Idol* and *Friends* are gems
for which my eBay readers eagerly
outbid each other. I promise my fans
that even I don't keep copies. They can
rest assured they own the only
volumes of one-of-a-kind manuscripts.
No more readings for me, no more lipstick.

No more readings for me, no more lipstick.
Now my persona depends on a ghost-
like absence. I quit my teaching job, post-
poned any interviews. Louise Glück
tried to talk me out of obscurity.
Then she saw my eBay seller's profile—
five stars, 100 percent. *You're liable
to have copycats,* she sighed, pretty
sure most poets were looking for a way
out. My stock portfolio's flowering.
My poetry is still empowering
women. A poem's worth can triple in days.
The lucky gal who sells is out of debt
and can retire to a warm climate.

Lucky Me

For a while I hated myself for not making it in prose—with movie rights
and screen credits and meetings with stars and walk-on parts.
Maybe, my friend Michael says, I simply wasn't hungry enough.
But I was famished.
                    (I'd written two novels for adults and one for teens,
none of which were published with covers, artwork on the front
and blurbs on the back. They never were put on bookshelves
in libraries or in stores, never assigned a price or barcode,
never marked down or remaindered. I never signed a copy
or had someone come up to me to say, *Hey, I'm in the middle
of your novel—not bad.* The titles were *Precious Blood, That Song
You Know the One about Love,* and *A Girl's Best Friend.*
Each took me several years to finish. And there was a screenplay
called *Headlines,* a comedy about a weather girl in New York
and her crazy brother who wants to become famous, but he has no real talent
and is not a murderer or a winning pie-eating contestant
so he's pretty much screwed. I wrote that screenplay with Jim Fall
who had a great collection of movie posters and soundtracks—
when we got stuck in our plot, we'd get up and dance.
He later worked for Dolly Parton's production company
and let me Xerox copies of *Precious Blood* in Dolly's office,
on Dolly's dime. [I'm sorry, Dolly! I really thought the book
would sell and then there'd be a screenplay that Jim and I would write
and you'd have a big part and compose a song called "Precious Blood"
for the soundtrack and that was how I was going to pay you back.]
Jim went on to direct *Trick*—a great movie—and he's directing
now for TV. I went on to write *Pickles,* another screenplay, this one
about a mother and daughter who are accepted to college the same year
and even live in the same dorm. The mother gave up the daughter
who was adopted by another family—and the two figure out slowly
that they are related because they're in the same biology class.
This was a comedy too, or so I thought. Michael read it
and he said it made him laugh, even though the jokes
were a little broad and there were too many logic problems.
Jim had a boyfriend we were convinced would finance *Headlines,*
but their relationship fell apart, and *Headlines* was never made

or even optioned—otherwise I wouldn't be writing about it with such nostalgia
and regret. Our agent—one of Jim's friends, just starting out—
told me that maybe I should write a sample script for *Cheers*
or a new show she thought I'd like called *Roseanne*. I'd never seen *Cheers*,
but I wrote two *Roseanne* scripts, one having to do with D.J.
mauling Barbie dolls and another one about Roseanne having a crush
on Johnny Cash. Later there was an episode about Roseanne
having a thing for Wayne Newton, but I'd obviously picked the wrong celebrity
and was never hired. I also wrote a few episodes of *She TV*, a vehicle
for my friend who was a stand-up comic and wanted to be a VJ on VH1,
but they told her she didn't have big enough boobs. She used to joke,
Just tell me who to blow to get this job and I'll do it . . . a line I tried to use, too,
but by then I was mostly writing poetry and the joke fell flat,
the joke teller—me—more pathetic because she was just trying
to get published in tiny literary magazines with print runs of 200
rather than make hundreds of thousands of dollars. I also wrote
a few skits for *Wake Up, Jerusalem* for another friend who was also trying
to break into comedy or acting. But I didn't understand enough about Jewish
culture, so my punch lines were a bit off. I was typecast
in real life as the kooky best friend to women who would later go on to play
the kooky best friend in movies. Laura played Hal's best friend in *Shallow Hal*,
and Mindy played a schoolmarm in a Woody Allen film.
And I was always just that far removed, my nose so close I could sniff
each celebrity walk by. In 1986, I actually met Kevin Bacon at the premiere
for *Quicksilver*, his bicycle messenger movie. Michael was an assistant
to a talent agent and would get us tickets to go to events where we could eat
cold salmon and fancy cheeses for free. Kevin probably knew *Quicksilver*
was going to be a flop, but still he was upbeat and kind. He asked me what I did
for a living and I told him that I was a writer, which was stretching it
since at that point I was in grad school and teaching comp. *Screenplays?*
he asked, with what seemed like genuine interest. But Jim and I hadn't started
Headlines yet, so I said, *No, I'm a poet . . .* at which point he drifted away.
A few years earlier I'd met Julia Roberts at a party for *Star 80*
at Eric Roberts' apartment. Michael said, *Mark my words—*
she is going to be the next big thing. I talked to Julia for a while
and told Michael he was crazy. She was mousy. Her teeth seemed
much smaller, less white back then—I don't remember any kind of flashy smile.
Her hair was that color that wasn't blond or brown

and she seemed, well, dull. I predicted Madonna was a flash in the pan—
Cyndi Lauper was the real singer, a star with staying power.
I was proven wrong over and over again.)

                                    I remember eating
one particularly delicious lunch at my Bank of America temp desk—
soda crackers and seedless grapes
I'd lifted the night before at an event to promote *Stepping Out*,
a movie starring Liza Minnelli. Michael called to say he had two free tickets
to Tracey Ullman's one-woman show *The Big Love. I'll be there,* I said.
But I can't chat right now. It wasn't that my boss was around.
I didn't want to talk because I knew Liza would never read
my revised *Pickles* script and I didn't want any false hope.
I didn't want to talk because I was happy,
scribbling "Lucky Me," a new poem, on a crumpled *Stepping Out* party napkin
I'd fished out of the bottom of my Goodwill purse.

throwing the dice

Delta Flight 659

—to Sean Penn

I'm writing this on a plane, Sean Penn,
with my black Pilot Razor ballpoint pen.
Ever since 9/11, I'm a nervous flyer. I leave my Pentium
Processor in Florida so TSA can't x-ray my stanzas, penetrate
my persona. Maybe this should be in iambic pentameter,
rather than this mock sestina, each line ending in a Penn

variant. I convinced myself the ticket to Baghdad was too expensive.
I contemplated going as a human shield. I read, in open-
mouthed shock, that your trip there was a $56,000 expenditure.
Is that true? I watched you on *Larry King Live*—his suspenders
and tie, your open collar. You saw the war's impending
mess. My husband gambled on my penumbra

of doubt. *So you station yourself at a food silo in Iraq. What happens
to me if you get blown up?* He begged me to stay home, be his Penelope.
I sit alone in coach, but last night I sat with four poets, depending
on one another as readers, in a Pittsburgh café. I tried to be your pen
pal in 1987, not because of your pensive
bad boy looks, but because of a poem you'd penned

that appeared in an issue of *Frank.* I still see the poet in you, Sean Penn.
You probably think fans like me are your penance
for your popularity, your star bulging into a pentagon
filled with witchy wanna-bes and penniless
poets who waddle toward your icy peninsula
of glamour like so many menacing penguins.

But honest, I come in peace, Sean Penn,
writing on my plane ride home. I want no part of your penthouse
or the snowy slopes of your Aspen.
I won't stalk you like the swirling grime cloud over Pig Pen.
I have no script or stupendous
novel I want you to option. I even like your wife, Robin Wright Penn.

I only want to keep myself busy on this flight, to tell you of four penny-
loafered poets in Pennsylvania
who, last night, chomping on primavera penne
pasta, pondered poetry, celebrity, Iraq, the penitentiary
of free speech. And how I reminded everyone that Sean Penn
once wrote a poem. I peer out the window, caress my lucky pendant:

Look, Sean Penn, the clouds are drawn with charcoal pencils.
The sky is opening like a child's first stab at penmanship.
The sun begins to ripen orange, then deepen.

Dinner Party Horror

After dessert, my friends and I try to figure out the order in which we would die in a horror movie.

Stan, the aggressive male, would be murdered first. His macho-ness would lead him out into the woods or up into the attic, unprepared for what he'd find there. Chatty Peg would go next—too innocently boisterous. She'd walk right up to the killer and try to make friends. Then David would go, through no fault of his own, but because he's black—sorry to say, minorities never make it to the end of horror films. Susan would also meet a grisly fate because (she admits this herself) she's a bit of a slut and sluts are always punished in movies.

It's down to Mary and me—I think she'd be the lone survivor since she's the most likeable. She thinks I'd be the lone survivor since I'm the most likeable. And surely, if one of us were to die, it would be as she tried to save the other.

Then Stan says, *Before you start congratulating yourselves, remember, one of you two bitches has to be the killer.*

We are horrified. Did he really say *bitches?*

It's a joke, he assures us.

David chimes in, *It's definitely an outside killer. Not Mary or Denise.* Besides, Susan says her autopsy shows she was molested before she was butchered, so that means her killer was male, right?

Peg says *Wait!—maybe Stan stabbed his twin right off to fool us, and he's not really dead, but has been lurking as the killer in the movie all along.* Stan likes the idea of his character coming back in the final scene. David still thinks it's an outside job. Mary says the whole conversation is giving her the creeps. Anyway, she has to get up early in the morning. She gets up from the couch and reaches for her car keys.

Wait! Don't go out there alone!

I try to warn her, but she won't listen.

Hurricane Katrina

I used to think maybe you loved me, now baby I'm sure . . .

—KATRINA AND THE WAVES

George Bush doesn't care about black people.

—KANYE WEST

George Bush used to think,

        maybe.

                I loved babies. I loved,

                        sure.

        Maybe you loved George Bush.

                  Maybe

  people used to care about babies.

                Maybe babies used to be cared for

under black bushes.

        The black waves didn't care

                and went west.

      Maybe George was sure.

            George Bush doesn't wave.

Maybe babies don't care about people

           named George.

                Babies care about babies.

Babies used to be sure.

       Maybe now babies think,

          George Bush doesn't love.

  But now George Bush waves.

       I'm sure I don't love like a baby.

  Maybe you never cared.

        People used to love thinking,

    but now I'm not sure.

The Language Police

—*after Diane Ravitch's* The Language Police

The busybody (banned as sexist, demeaning to older women) who lives next door called my daughter a tomboy (banned as sexist) when she climbed the jungle (banned; replace with "rain forest") gym (alternative: replace "jungle gym" with "play structure"). Then she had the nerve to call her an egghead and a bookworm (both banned as offensive; replace with "intellectual") because she read fairy (banned because it suggests homosexuality; replace with "elf") tales.

I'm tired of the Language Police turning a deaf ear (banned as handicapism) to my complaints. I'm no Pollyanna (banned as sexist) and will not accept any lame (banned as offensive; replace with "walks with a cane") excuses this time.

If Alanis Morissette can play God (banned) in *Dogma* (banned as ethnocentric; replace with "Doctrine" or "Belief"), why can't my daughter play stickball (banned as regional or ethnic bias) on boys' night out (banned as sexist)? Why can't she build a snowman (banned, replace with "snow person") without that fanatic (banned as ethnocentric; replace with "believer," "follower," or "adherent") next door telling her she's going to go to hell (banned; replace with "heck" or "darn")?

Do you really think this is what the Founding Fathers (banned as sexist; replace with "the Founders" or "the Framers") had in mind? That we can't even enjoy our devil (banned)-ed ham sandwiches in peace? I say put a stop to this cult (banned as ethnocentric) of PC old wives' tales (banned as sexist; replace with "folk wisdom") and extremist (banned as ethnocentric; replace with "believer," "follower," or "adherent") conservative duffers (banned as demeaning to older men).

As an heiress (banned as sexist; replace with "heir") to the First Amendment, I feel that only a heretic (use with caution when comparing religions) would try to stop American vernacular from flourishing in all its inspirational (banned as patronizing when referring to a person with disabilities) splendor.

Repeat

Pete and Repeat sat on a fence.
Pete fell off and who was left?
This was my first joke. I'd tell it to my little sister
who didn't know at first what "repeat" meant.

Pete fell off and who was left?
I'd taunt her. *Shut up!* she'd scream, knowing what was next.
She learned what "repeat" meant
from a hostile kindergarten comedian.

I'd taunt her. *Shut up!* she'd scream. And I knew what was next.
My father would separate us—his preschooler
from his hostile kindergarten comedian.
We sat on opposite ends of the couch, not allowed to talk.

My father would separate us, as though his preschooler
were Pete, his kindergartener Repeat. It was torture
sitting on opposite ends of the couch, not allowed to talk.
I mouthed the setup of the joke

to my sister who bunched her eyes closed. I tortured
her, outsmarting my father. Technically I wasn't talking.
I only *mouthed* the setup of the joke,
until he caught me, until he said, *So you think that's funny?*

I was proud, outsmarting my father. Technically I wasn't talking
when I stuck out my tongue in my sister's direction
until he caught me, until he said, *So you think that's funny?*
Look what you've done. Now she's crying.

Did you stick out your tongue? It was a direct question,
but I pleaded the Fifth. My mother said she'd had it with us.
Look what you've done. Now Mommy's crying,
my sister lisped. Then she asked: *What came first the chicken or the egg?*

I pleaded the Fifth. My mother said she'd had it with us,
my sister's and my exhausting infinite loops.
My sister asked, *No, really . . . What came first the chicken or the egg?*
I pretended there was an answer, but that I wouldn't tell her.

I figured out how to stop the exhausting infinite loop
just by changing the joke's first line.
Then there'd just be one answer, and the joke would be over.
Pete and Tickle-My-Feet were sitting on a fence . . .

Just by changing the joke's first line,
I was able to get my sister to invite me to fondle her toes.
Pete and Tickle-My-Feet were sitting on a fence,
I'd say and she'd run in the other direction.

Only once was I able to get my sister to invite me to fondle her toes.
I don't know why you're such a bully,
my mother'd say and I'd run in the other direction.
I never told her about my cousin's peanut can with the pop-up snake.

My father didn't know why I was such a bully.
I never told him about how my cousin held me hostage with a water pistol,
how he tricked me into opening his peanut can with the pop-up snake.
My sister started telling jokes to the smaller neighborhood kids.

I held a water pistol to my sister's temple.
I'm only joking around, I'd tell my little sister
who started singling out the smaller neighborhood kids:
Pete and Repeat sat on a fence . . .

Basically

Basically, there are two kinds of children:
those who like to torture and those who like to rescue.
Most get their first practice on insects—
some save ants in a jar with breathing holes punched
in the lid and feed them crumbled saltines and sugar.
Some pin a ladybug under the magnifying glass
and wait for the sun to burst it into flames.
Some rip off spiders' legs. Some make tiny spider-sized casts
and crutches and wheelchairs. These children usually progress
quickly to animals and birds. Some fire at pigeons
with BB guns. Some take the pigeons home
swaddled in T-shirts or socks and try to mend the wounds
with Band Aids or maybe gauze and masking tape.
Some pluck out a cat's entire set of whiskers
and laugh as it bumps into chairs like a drunk.
Some make a papoose and carry the cat around
to save it embarrassment. Some like to chop off
the legs of frogs. Some like to set frogs free.
At night all children are exhausted by the cruelties
of the world and fight sleep because there is still
so much to do. So many tiny slings to be sewn,
tailored to fit around a puppy's neck and front leg.
So many slingshots to be fired. The Y
held tightly, a secret in every bully's fist.

A Dog and a Boy

A mother, her five children, and a grandma stop us on the boardwalk where dogs are forbidden. A clump of dappled fur strains against its collar. It is late at night—the children should be in bed. Nick and I should be in bed, but we can't sleep. The mother is frantic and points to a motel down a side street. *We are paying weekly,* she says, *and the landlord just found out about our dog.* A little girl with Down syndrome pokes my breast and barks. A grandma is holding the leash of what she claims is a Lhasa apso. *Our dog needs a home or we'll be kicked out,* the mother pleads as little boys crowd behind us, and I feel as though we are back on the train in Paris where the gypsies (I mean, the *gens du voyage*—traveling people—as they are called in France) stole our bag with our money and passports. Nick reaches for his back pocket and keeps his hand on his wallet. *I'm allergic to dogs,* I say. *But where will we live now?* the mother whimpers, and one of the boys begins to wail as though on cue. *Our dog is a good dog, very good with children. We don't want him to end up in the pound. I paid $500 for him, but . . .* The grandma holds her heart and moans. Nick says, *I'm sorry—we aren't allowed to have pets in our condo.* We know it's a scam, so we keep walking, past the Edy's Ice Cream where the owner with the bleached bouffant and skinny rainbow eyebrows is lugging in her inflatable four-foot cone, past Mamacita's restaurant where two waiters pull the life-sized statue of a man in a blanket poncho and sombrero up the stairs. The metal shutters on the T-shirt shops are all coming down. The waves break, but it's so dark we can only see the white disembodied caps. Maybe the gypsies (I mean, the Romany, as they are now called here in the states) stole the dog from someone else. Maybe there are "missing dog" signs up in shops and on telephone poles. Maybe the gypsies planned to keep our $400 and then call the police to turn us in for a reward from the real owners. *I doubt that was even a purebred,* Nick says, making sure he still has our keys.

❖ ❖ ❖

When we first moved to Florida we were given a phone number that used to belong to Elsa and her son Bobby. Elsa's boyfriend would call collect from the Miami Correctional Facility and leave messages on our machine. *Baby, come on. Please pick up.* He'd call three or four times a week: *Elsa, don't give up on me. . . . Hey, Elsa, it'll hurt you more than me if you hold a grudge, you know I'm sorry. . . . Elsa, I just want to check how you and Bobby are doing. Come visit, OK?* Maybe Elsa stopped in to see him on her own and to give him her new number, or maybe he just gave up. But now Bobby's in trouble: *This is the Broward School System letting you know*

Bobby wasn't in school three times this week. . . . Bobby is having behavioral problems in math class. . . . Bobby is habitually late and failing. If there isn't significant improvement, he'll have to stay back. I call to say we are not Bobby's parents, that Bobby and Elsa have forgotten to update their information. No, I don't know where they are. No, I can't give them a message since I've never even met them. The principal says he just wants someone to be responsible. Then a few weeks later another call—it's parent/teacher night. We are nervous. We know the teachers will want to know about the problems we have at home. We'll have to explain that there'll be new rules for Bobby now—homework before dinner, and no caffeinated drinks allowed. I straighten Nick's tie. I ask him if my skirt is too short. We want to make a good impression. It is time to find our ghost boy and take him home.

Apple

My friend was exasperated—*I can't deal anymore,*
she said, leaving me in the Holiday Inn lobby
with her first-grader and his Spiderman backpack.

My godson had missed a lot of school
because of the separation, the restraining order,
the bad nights of sleep at the hotel,

the cough syrup, the bolted door.
My friend needed her son
with her as she went to the lawyer's office,

the safety deposit box, the Starbucks
where she wept and blew her nose into grainy napkins.
Now it was time for his homework

that he slid from his backpack
with a curt note: *Patrick has missed*
six days. Please have him finish these worksheets

in an attempt to catch up. Sincerely, Mrs. Harris.
We counted six pieces of paper.
Patrick, can you write your name on this line?

He took the pencil into his fist.
He was fine until the "K," which he wrote backward.
He furiously erased, almost ripping through the paper.

The worksheets were about the short A,
the way it sounds. *Hey,* I said, *Patrick has a short A in it.*
and so does Mrs. Harris. I repeated their names

until I thought he got it—*Patrick, Harris,*
exasperated, can't, bad, napkins, catch, man, backward . . .
Circle the pictures of things with the short A sound:

A truck, a hat, a bee. Patrick went to circle the bee,
but I lifted his hand, the pencil point hovering
over the paper. *What sounds the most like Patrick?*

Hat, Patrick, Harris, I said, a big hint.
Oh yeah, he said. *Yeah,* I said. *Hear that short A sound. Yeah?*
I'm hungry, Patrick yawned, telling me how in the morning

there would be free muffins here, and hardboiled eggs.
I looked at my watch. It was almost eight.
Patrick was supposed to be in bed by 8:30,

though he hadn't had a regular schedule for a while.
I thought of putting him in his booster seat,
trying to find a restaurant with takeout

but the homework loomed. He was starting to close
his bloodshot eyes. *I know where the vending machine is,*
he said, then he led me to it, his papers still spread out

on the table where he'd have his breakfast.
I bought him a granola bar and Sun Chips, E8, B4,
which seemed slightly healthier than the Snickers he wanted.

We watched his dinner plummet. He pushed
the metal door open and pulled out the snacks from the bin.
I slid in a dollar for water. The sound

of the dropping bottle startled him.
It's OK, I said, though nothing was really OK.
He didn't talk about his father or what he'd done.

We went back to his homework.
Backpack has two short A's. Can you hear that?
I exaggerated the A's, repeating the word.

Patrick, Harris, backpack, hat, snacks . . .
Think, I said, *before you circle the next picture.*
I have to confess I gave him a lot of clues.

I couldn't bear to see him erase,
I couldn't bear to say the word "wrong."
He circled the map, the basket, the jacks.

Then a strange request: DRAW A PICTURE
OF YOUR FAVORITE CAT. A blank square
looming. Patrick scribbled something

so tiny and fierce I didn't question it. His face
was full of crumbs. The final worksheet,
Three Apples. The directions read: COLOR EACH APPLE

A DIFFERENT COLOR—YELLOW, GREEN, AND RED.
Patrick dumped the contents of his crayon box
and we found a yellow stub, a green stick

with the paper curled off. Not exactly apple green,
though it would do. Patrick began to cry
when we couldn't find a red.

I dumped out the contents of my purse,
hoping for a red felt tip. We went to the front desk—
Do you have a red pen? The woman

behind the counter checked all the drawers,
but she was sorry. It was already past bedtime—
Patrick was whimpering, his nose running.

I wondered if I should go to find a Walgreen's.
I have an idea, I said, *You can color the apple pink
and I'll write a note to Mrs. Harris telling her*

it was late and we couldn't find a red crayon.
Pink is for girls, Patrick wailed.
What about purple? I said. *Purple is red with blue in it.*

No no no. He kicked and stomped,
wanting me to take him back to his house
where he knew he could find a red crayon,

where he could find his favorite pillow
and toy box and hotdogs and buns.
But there were also guns and an angry man.

I held him until he stopped kicking,
until he snapped *fine.* He scrawled
a few purple loopy marks that went

outside the lines. Each apple had oval eyes
and a U-shaped smile that seemed to mock us.
I wrote a note to Mrs. Harris explaining

Patrick's crayon situation, which I hoped explained
the whole situation. The whites of Patrick's eyes
were full of red squiggles. I put the papers

back in his folder and zipped up his backpack.
I carried him up the elevator to the dark hotel room
where my friend was under the covers—exhaustion.

I could see Patrick's clothes in a heap on the floor.
Somewhere in that shadowed pile were his pajamas,
but by now he was snoring. I positioned him

in the bed next to his mother's, sliding off
his Spiderman sneakers, then pulling the covers up
to his chin. *Did you wash his face? Brush his teeth?*

my friend mumbled. *Yes,* I lied.
I left the key card on the bureau and backed out—
free, relieved, but haunted, probably like Patrick's dad.

That asshole. That bastard. That bad, bad apple.

Stupid Vanilla

In college, I was hired by a couple to take care of their two boys after school until the workday was over. In return, I got a room in the attic. One boy was ten, another four. The little one suffered from asthma and had already figured out the manipulation that some sick children master. He could wheeze or choke on cue—whenever he didn't want to pick up his toys. Whenever he didn't want to sit with me to go over the flashcards his parents made him practice so he'd be a star next year in the best private kindergarten, so he could get into the best private middle school, then into the best private high school, and then into Harvard or Yale, like his mother and father, respectively. The two practiced law in the city and came back to the suburbs around ten or eleven each night, even though when I was hired they said they'd be home at six, seven the latest. They fired the house-keeper the first week I was there, so I was also making the kids' dinner. The maid told me that on her last job she'd been thrown down the stairs by Tina Louise, the glamour-puss from *Gilligan's Island*. I told her she should go to the police, but she was afraid. Who would they believe? An illegal from Guatemala or Ginger?

On Saturdays, the mother asked me to help with the laundry. I folded stacks of little shirts and pants then drove her to the dry cleaner and supermarket. She wore several different wigs, which fascinated me—one was long and straight, another short and curly, and a third was a reddish pageboy. I wondered if she confused the jury with her different hairstyles. I wondered how often she went to court.

I was very afraid of the husband who told the wife what to wear and had the habit of calling her fat, which she wasn't. He also called the ten-year-old porky. He'd hurl a Nerf ball at the boy when he was daydreaming—which was often—and when his son didn't catch it, the father would shake his head and walk away. I knew I was the next one on his list to be singled out, so I sucked in my stomach whenever I passed him. When the jalopy they lent me to take the little one to preschool broke down, the father said I had to walk him there. The school was a mile away and the boy was allergic to everything in the fall air. When he started gasping and his inhaler didn't work, I picked him up and carried him. I asked the father when the car would be fixed, and he said he was going to junk it and, let's face it, the walk would do me good. He couldn't let me use his car because it was custom—not even his wife was allowed to touch it. I began to tell him about his son's asthma attack and he said, *Not now.*

The older boy came into my room with his friends and scratched up all my records playing DJ. The little boy took to calling me Stupid Vanilla, even in front of his parents who—could I have been imagining this?—both, without much success, tried to stifle their laughter. Then the father said, *That's not nice, son. Don't call people stupid.* And the wife chuckled at his bad sitcom line. A few days later the dishwasher broke and he complained that I hadn't washed the glasses well enough, that I shouldn't leave them in the strainer to dry or they'd streak. He flung a kitchen towel toward me. When I didn't catch it, it draped over my sneaker.

The mother said, *Your typing is keeping us up at night. Can you find another time to do your homework, hon?*

I tried to tell the wife that it was too much work, that this wasn't our agreement, that I'd missed a few classes because she wasn't home when she said she would be and I couldn't leave the kids alone. She promised she'd get home earlier next week, that she'd hire another housekeeper soon. Then she handed me a stack of envelopes—*Would you mind taking these to the post office?* I was sick of cutting up hot dogs on plates, of tripping on toys, of trying to stay out of the father's way. I moved out all my stuff one morning—the kids at school, the parents at work, the time I loved their big opulent house best. I wrote a resignation letter and left it on a table in the hall. The mother tracked me down through school to accuse me of child abuse, stealing one of her necklaces. She reminded me that she was a lawyer, that I couldn't get away with this. Then she broke into a sob. *He's going to kill me—can't you come back? Please? At least for another week?*

I wonder if that family ever talks about their disastrous 1985 nanny, that lazy white bitch who thought she was too good to pick up their socks.

small tip

"Please Don't Sit Like a Frog, Sit Like a Queen"

graffiti inside the cubicle of a ladies' bathroom
in a university in the Philippines

Remember to pamper, remember to preen.
The world doesn't reward a pimply girl.
Don't sit like a frog, sit like a queen.

Buy a shampoo that gives your locks sheen.
If your hair is straight, get it curled.
Remember to pamper, remember to preen.

Keep your breath minty and your teeth white and clean.
Paint your nails so they glisten, ten pearls.
Don't sit like a frog, sit like a queen.

Smile, especially when you're feeling mean.
Keep your top down when you take your car for a whirl.
Remember to pamper, remember to preen.

Don't give into cravings, you need to stay lean
so you can lift up your skirt as you prance and twirl.
Don't sit like a frog, sit like a queen.

Don't marry the professor, marry the dean.
Marry the king, don't marry the earl.
Remember to pamper, remember to preen.
Don't sit like a frog, sit like a queen.

I Dreamed I Wrote This Sestina Wearing My Maidenform Bra

In the thirties, A-cup breasts were called nubbins,
B cups snubbins,
C cups droopers, and D cups super droopers.
In the fifties, a bullet bra could make a bombshell
of most women. Pointy torpedo cups
had every Hollywood starlet hooked.

But Tinkerbell was only a 32-A, flitting past Captain Hook,
Peter Pan admiring her nubbins
as he cupped
her in his hands and snubbed
adulthood. When he dropped a bombshell—
that he wanted to be a boy forever—she drooped

in his palm, wishing for a padded bra, her eyes drooping
too.
         Snow White was a respectable 36-B, just enough to hook
the prince without being tawdry. Snow was a bombshell,
though, to the dwarves, little nubbins
of men she snubbed
without meaning to, filling their tiny cups

with grape juice instead of wine. A couple
of times she even mixed up their names.
                          Cinderella drooped
until her fairy godmother found her the right bra. Snubbing
her flat-chested stepsisters, Cinderella hooked
herself into one sturdy 38-C underwire and two luscious nubs
emerged through her ragged blouse. The bombshell

of the ball, she was afraid to drop a bombshell
on Prince Charming, that she'd be cupping
well water and cleaning cinders by morning, nubbins
of pollen and feathers stuck in the straw of her droopy
broom.
         Sleeping Beauty almost looked like a hooker
with those 40-D knockers that seemed to snub

the wicked fairy's saggy cleavage. Sleeping Beauty didn't want to snub
the old women who asked her to help spin, so the bombshell
pricked her finger, fulfilling the fairy's spell. The hook-
up with the prince wouldn't come for one hundred years, but that was only a hiccup
of time to SB, who slept through the century. All the tulips drooped
toward her to whisper into the pink nubbins

of her ears: *Never snub your dreams, drink from the cup*
of your bombshelled unconscious, where para-droopers
unhook nubbins of meaning as you snooze in your Maidenform Bra.

What Women Know

When the moderator asked us during the poetry reading's Q&A:
What do women know that men don't? I froze, then made a joke,
Well, there is one crucial thing, but I'm not going to be the one
to give it away . . .
                              I thought of my friend Jo who betrayed us all
by telling the boys about *It's Fun to be a Girl!* Jo was paid
in nickels to whisper the secrets of blood and white pads, pink
sanitary belts that looked like garters. The boys were grossed out and overused
the word "period" and "cramp" to embarrass us. *Don't write too fast—*
you might get a CRAMP. Wonder what we'll do in class next PERIOD.
Ha ha ha. Thanks a lot, Jo. She shrugged, wanting to be a boy
not a girl, hoping her period would never come
if she refused training bras and *Tiger Beat* and the pocketbooks
the rest of us carried with our Modess tucked inside so we'd be ready
when those first drops dribbled during math class or history
or science, we couldn't be sure. Jo wouldn't answer
to her birth name Jo Ann and wore overalls and baseball caps
that read Allied Auto because her father worked there as a mechanic
and got them for free.
                              I said something like *I believe gender is a construct,*
and luckily for me the other poet on stage agreed,
and the audience nodded as though I were making some kind of sense.
Still, the moderator's question haunted me. Was there really something
I knew that I didn't even know I knew? Was there something
he and the male poet on stage knew that I didn't?
                                                      The next morning
I took a walk through Houston before I left for the airport.
I was the only pedestrian except for a barefoot drag queen
in front of the pink Taco Cabana who asked, *Honey,*
do you have any change for the bus? She'd had a tough night, I could tell—
her chin was full of stubble, her pageboy wig askew.
Before I gave her the quarters that jangled in my trousers,
I wanted to ask her, *What do women know that men don't?*
But just as I was about to pose the question, she belched, a sound
somewhere between a man burp and woman burp, a sour cloud.
I walked on and bought the *New York Times* and read a story

about how soon Big Apple residents will be able to change
their genders on their birth certificates
whether they've had sex-change surgery or not.

And there was my answer—

another case of *l'esprit de l'escalier*. If only
I could have referenced the article last night to make my point.
If only I'd whipped out my Florida license, the big M
crouched in the sex square. After standing in line for six hours
at the DMV, I came home to a tentative voice on my answering machine:
Please check your license, we may have made a mistake
concerning your gender. If the information is correct, please ignore this message.
If not, please come back tomorrow . . . You could tell the caller
didn't want to offend—she was an F
or at least sounded like one over the phone. I imagined
the cubicle where she passed around my photo—*does this look*
like a transvestite to you? Does anyone remember taking this picture?
Did she seem like a "real" woman?

Ah, staircase wit.

What I should have said to the moderator:
I'm sorry, I'm unqualified to answer the question.
I've been a man since 2000. There's no way
I'm going to wait in that long line again, just to be a gal.

Girl Talk

I lost my Ronnie when I was only fifty-eight. Fifty-eight! Can you imagine? I was so young then, but I wasn't interested in anyone else. I often fantasized that Ronnie died (I know, terrible!) but then when he really did die (heart) I missed him so much. About a year later, a man tried to touch me at a party (a retirement party for Lulu's husband, Ralph). I slapped him and went home crying before they even served the cake. I spent a decade crying. I didn't even touch myself, if you know what I mean. My daughter gave me this—I don't know what it's called—a dildo maybe? It was purple, and it scared me to death! But then, when I was sixty-eight, I met Herbert (at the community center—I was volunteering and he came in asking if there were any regular card games). I don't know why I went out with him—perhaps because he seemed very gentle. After our date (Giorgio's—I had the flounder, a little dry, but OK, and very nice bread) he asked me back to his condo (Sea Towers, eighth floor, ocean view, very neat) to watch a movie (Turner Classics). Then, after an hour or so, he told me he had a second TV in his bedroom and asked me to lie down with him there. I said, *Are you crazy? This is our first date . . .* and he said, *But I have prostate problems. Really, all I want to do is lie down and hold you.* Well, I was hooked. We've been together for over ten years. No sex! He just kisses me (no tongue even) and rubs my back. His doctor wanted to give him Viagra, but I told him, *Herbert, you get those pills and it's all over.* He's not interested, really, either. Sometimes we stay up all night listening to records (he still has a stereo that works) and holding hands. It's incredible. I feel like a schoolgirl again.

Cinderella's Ghost Slipper

ghost word: a word that has come into a dictionary,
grammar, or fable as a result of a mistranslation or
misinterpretation

The first Cinderella (Yen-Shen) was Chinese
and had the smallest toes in all the land. Her feet were bound,
not with glass, but by magic slippers
made from the bones of her dead pet fish.

An Egyptian Cinderella had rose-red shoes, made of gold
mixed with iron. An Arcadian Cinderella named Jouanah
got her ballroom pumps from a cow (who used to be her mother
until mom turned herself into a bovine to help with the harvest).

An Algonquin Cinderella benefited from the Invisible Hunter
who transformed her tattered moccasins with new beads.
Zezolla (Cat Cinderella) lost a scruffy overshoe,
but still the prince was intrigued. And Jerry Lewis

in *Cinderfella* leaves behind a stinky loafer
as a keepsake for his princess-to-be.
Indian Cinduri didn't lose a shoe at all,
but an anklet for the prince to ponder in his palm.

Korean Kongjee escaped not only a wicked stepmother,
but death itself. Shoeless, she climbed a rope up to heaven.
Finette turned her body into a bear and still
the prince discovered her. Donkey Skin dropped her ring

into cake batter and the Many-Furred Creature
tossed hers into soup, both leaving clues for their princes
to chomp and spit out. And before Perrault and Disney
softened the blow, elder stepsisters, trying to get the prince,

cut off their toes, their heels, their bunions
filling Cinderella's slipper with blood.
Perrault, it is sometimes argued, was mistranslated—
that Cendrillon's shoes were fur slippers

(pantoufle de vair) and not glass slippers
(pantoufle de verre) at all. So the ghost of the animal
lives in the glassblower's breath, the way a dead
parent lives on in the tree, the fruit, the cow,

the goldfish, the candle, the eggplant, the fairy godmother.
And Cinderella herself is a ghost to Askungen,
Ceniceinta, Aschenbrödel, Assepoester,
every Harlequin heroine, Vasilisa the Beautiful,

Kao, Abadeha, Cam, Parnette, The She-Bear,
Ash Girl, Cinderbutt, and "A Young Girl
Nicknamed 'Ass Hide' Who Got Married
with the Help of Little Ants." It was not always

happily-ever-after for Cinderella. Poor Oona,
an Irish Cinderella, was swallowed by a whale,
subsequent to her prince finding her
via a countrywide scavenger shoe hunt.

And long ago, before she became so magnanimous,
Cinderella and the prince, for amusement,
forced those mean stepsisters to dance in red-hot metal boots
heated in the fire and delivered with tongs.

Spoon

John Updike's image stays with me—his male character admires a slender
young woman whose collarbones strain toward each other and almost meet
in a dip in which he envisions placing a teaspoon. I can't help but think

that this lovely girl could not let herself eat whatever was once in that spoon
on the spoon rest of her throat, whatever was cooking in her body that became
a willowy stove. I imagine the most expensive of silver teaspoons, perhaps

the handle monogrammed with her family's initials, lying there like a necklace
without a chain. No matter how much I suck air into my throat, I can't
make a hollow place for a spoon on my neck. I can't even really see

my collarbones unless I hunch my shoulders and roll them forward.
I wasn't ever exquisitely delicate, but I don't blame John Updike for that.
To this day, I look for women with teaspoon indentations and admire them

like Updike's character did. He moves on to other descriptions—the girl
in the supermarket with ice-cream-scoop breasts. Sometimes before I take a bite
of something sweet, I use my spoon as an upside down mirror.

Perimenopause

Last night I dreamed that I used a knife instead of a spoon to take my first bite of morning yogurt and the blade cut right into my tongue. The yogurt mixed with my blood like acrylics. I put a paintbrush right in my mouth and swirled! Then I started painting everything pink. The tablecloth, the water glass, the coffee cup, the bowl, the innocent spoon. If the teeth are male, then the tongue is a young girl. You may suspect the mouth is the vagina and you may be right. You may think a hole in the hand is stigmata, but according to my dream book, it's also a vagina—unless the hole is on the back of the hand, in which case it's an anus. And blood from the mouth/vagina? Well, I haven't had my period in four months. If you think people start to zone out when you tell them about your periods, try telling them about menopause. They tend to yawn, their mouths, little vaginas, little drowsy moist caves. Oh white yogurt, I suspect I know what you are.

The Da Vinci Poke

My husbAND Nick says *if Ron Howard REAlly wanted to shock the Vatican*
there shoulD have been a sex scene betWeen Tom Hanks and Audrey Tautou,
the supposed descendent of Mary Magdalene and Jesus Christ.
I say *Da Vinci Does Dallas?* and Nick says
OR what about the The Da Vinci PoKe?

Ron Jeremy as Robert Langdon
and Jenna Jameson as Sophie Neveu
search for The Da VINci Bunghole Code,
an ancient cryptex of long-since-forgotten sexual positions.
Jeremy AND Jameson do it in sacred places along the way—

Westminster Abbey, Saint-Sulpice, Temple Church,
beside tombs, in pews, on altars, even in the Louvre.
Jameson, not reaLIzing at first who she really is,
assumes that everyone can levitate while coming
or change water into scented lubricants.

Opus Dei, the ones who live among the shadows,
in our version, are Opus Gay, a cult into whipping
and boNDAge. Silas, the albino monk, played by Chad Slater,
kills the uptight Sister Sandrine, played by Xaviera Hollander,
a happy hooker turned bed-and-breakfast entrepreneur.

She's perfect for the press junket and traveLs
along with Slater, who claims to have had an affair
with Tom Cruise. Bob Guccione is cast as Sir Leigh Teabing,
the aging OVEr-the-top wealthy historian. Traci Lords
steaLs each of her supporting ACtrEss scenes as the butler Remy,

who nicknames her boss "Sir Teabag."
Nick and I give ourselves walk-on parts as a pRiESTand a nun
protesting IN the first scene at the book signing.
And *The Da Vinci Poke* ends with Jameson giving birth—
how could it not?—a holy child visited by three porno kings

(Long Dong Silver, Goldstein, and Flynt), and a donkey,
making a cameo from its show in Nuevo Laredo. And finally,
thanks to Nick and me, a triple-X movie
dEAls with the big questions: When is nudity
museum worthy? When is it crass? What is sacred?

What is profane? What is kitsch and what is art?
Unscrambled, *The Da Vinci Poke* becomes "a hot pink deviCE"
and *The Da Vinci Code* becomes "the candid voice."
Finally, thanks to us, a triple-X movie for brainiacs
who get off on a tight hard plot.

THE DA VINCI POKE's OWN SECRET CODE:
Andrea Dworkin and Linda Lovelace Rest in Peace

No Home-Wrecker

When I was twenty, I kissed a man
much older than I was. My drunk hand found
a strange indent and lump of flesh
on the back of his waist, an extra little potbelly.
I quickly moved my fingers away and grabbed
onto his shoulder instead. After the kiss,
the man immediately told me he was married. For years
my memory told me that I slapped him and left the party,
a friend's cramped Beacon Hill apartment.
But now I think I remember what happened—
he began to cry, just slightly, so that at first
I thought his wet eyes had something to do with an allergy.
Then he said he really loved his wife and needed
air. We took baby steps, holding hands,
through the slippery cobblestone streets,
snow settling on my eyelashes, in his beard.
We slipped into a diner where our coats and scarves
dripped puddles onto the floor.
He told me a long story about married life—
her chemotherapy, how he'd just lost his job.
I sobered up and looked at my plate of pale scrambled eggs,
what I imagined cancer looked like,
what I imagined fat looked like under the skin.
I poked my fork around, curious now
to see that spare tire, that love handle of his.
He kept blowing his nose, his cheeks fat and pink
like the soles of a newborn's feet.
The rest of him looked lean in his woolly sweater,
then he seemed to shrink even smaller
as he put back on his oversized overcoat to walk me home.
I felt rejected when he left me at my door
and disappeared into a flurry, thanking me for listening.
The story I told my friends who were at the party
was that OK, he was kind of cute, but I was
no home-wrecker. The story I told myself
was that I'd have never done anything like that—

his wife had cancer for god's sake.
Now that I look back, the man was probably only
in his late thirties, about the age I am now.
He had no money so I wound up covering our diner check,
emptying the last of my change on the table for too small a tip.

one-armed
bandits

Casino

When my sister says *there's been an accident,* I think *car,* then *bus,* but she says *no, escalator* and *pile up.*

When my sister says the word *mother* and *scalped,* I think cowboys and Indians, tiny shrunken heads, the blood all boiled out, warpaths.

When my sister says the word *father* and *collapsed,* I turn the TV sound down. It's Thursday morning, September 11, 2003—the memorial, the reading of names. I had planned to go to BJ's and Publix today, shop for a dinner party tomorrow.

It happened yesterday, Mom was in surgery for a very long time. . . . The hospital is just calling now.

Atlantic City, my sister says, *I can drive there in four or five hours.* I tell her I can fly. I hang up. Nick gets online. He finds a direct flight on Spirit.

I remember my mother telling my sister and me to braid our hair before riding the Ferris wheel and a story about a girl's loose curls flying into the gears, being torn out in chunks, her blood, warm red specks, dripping onto the seats below. And how the carnie had to stop the ride with a jolt and how a fireman shot up in a bucket truck with a pair of scissors to release the screaming girl. When the ride went back on, the passengers got off, one by one, no one smiling or laughing any more. And I was never sure if my mother was on that ride or in the park that day or if it was just a story she liked to tell. The girl's hair scattered, whipping by the horses in the merry-go-round, twisting into the cotton candy.

And my mother's hair, also left behind in some gear, her blood soaking the silver escalator steps, the casino carpet.

Up and down and round and round. All the bald lemons and cherries spinning.

My Mother's Hair

My mother's "fall" on its Styrofoam head, the shiny chestnut *That Girl* flip that she wore out to dinner with her Fabergé perfume, which came in a glass bottle with a tiger fur cap. I couldn't help but make little fingernail moons in the Styrofoam, whole eyebrows and lashes. The blank face scared me—it was the bumpy face of nightmares, monsters, people disappearing. I was glad when my mother put it away, into the shiny tube-shaped case that I used for my 45s after her "fall" went out of style.

She also had a two-foot blond braid that my sister wore with her gold-beaded unitard for her modern jazz recital and I wore to a B-52s concert a few years later, swinging it around as I danced, afraid it might fall off and I'd lose it, the stunning synthetic snake.

My mother trusted her real hair to Roger, whose beauty parlor had an entrance in Massachusetts and an exit in Rhode Island. I'd run back and forth through both doors playing fugitive until he sat me down with his hardcover books of glamorous bouffants. I'd lose myself in the swirling curls of the models in the beauty parlor paintings with bamboo frames that hung over the chairs in his waiting room. My mother seemed so much smaller when her hair was wet. The hairdryers looked like astronauts' helmets. I was mesmerized by the black combs that bobbed in aqua Barbercide.

I miss my mother's hair—her fake hair, her real hair, her teased hair, her perms. My mother gives me her headbands and bobby pins, saying, *I won't be using these anymore.* I miss my mother's hair paraphernalia—the rinses, the rollers, the AquaNet, the pin curls, the clear rain bonnet that folded into what looked like a tiny suitcase and disappeared.

Moonprint

My father zigzagged down the hall. He couldn't find the bedroom and he wouldn't accept my help. His fever was rising—a staph infection—but I didn't know that yet. I thought he just was disoriented, post-traumatic stress. I was afraid he'd fall, his coccyx bone to the wooden floor, if he misjudged the edge of the mattress, where, before the accident, he kneeled every night to say his prayers, whispering the rosary, crossing himself, his knees on the wooden floor even though he's seventy-six. It wasn't really praying unless he was uncomfortable, back straight, no elbows leaning on the bed. The brown leather slippers we bought him for Christmas were precarious and loose on his feet, which made me even more nervous. I'd give him glasses of water, but he'd sneak into the bathroom and splash the water into the sink. He wouldn't drink and he wouldn't eat. Just home from the hospital, he sat in his favorite rocking chair, unable to follow the conversation. He shivered in a sweater, although the rest of us were fanning ourselves.

I didn't know what was happening under his sleeve, the red streak of staph shooting from the inside of his wrist through his blood stream, up his arm and right toward his heart. He wouldn't let me wash him or see his body. I bought disposable washcloths we warmed in the microwave so he could sit and wash himself on a chair I dragged into the bathroom. My mother let me help her shower, but my father was extremely private. It wasn't until I felt his forehead, feverish under my fingertips, that I took his temperature—104 degrees—and my sister and her husband rushed him to the emergency room where a nurse peeled off his sweater and gasped at his Magic Marker line.

After he was admitted, I went to the hospital while my mother's friend from the quilting group stayed with her at home. A doctor wrapped herself up in what looked like a clear plastic poncho. I could see the sweat on her forehead when she put a PICC line in. Blood pooled on the towels under my father, droplets splashed up and onto her goggles, and I said, *Dad, look at me,* as the doctor snaked a catheter into his elbow-pit, up his arm, following the curve of his shoulder, which would send antibiotics from an IV right to his heart. My mother couldn't come visit my father because she wasn't supposed to expose her scalp to germs. It was hard for her to stay home in her bandages and kerchief.

Though my father had been pale, a greenish gray, his cheeks turned pink a few minutes after the first of the antibiotics were squirted into him. The doctor stripped off her plastic gear and gave me gloves and showed me how to attach the bags of antibiotics to the PICC so that when he was released in a few days I'd know how to inject him. I dialed the phone in my father's hospital room so that he could talk to my mother. Then I called every fifteen minutes to see how she was doing. Finally her friend said, *I can take care of her, I promise!* I gave my mother's friend my cell number even though the hospital sign said NO CELL PHONES PLEASE.

My dad's eyes were alert again and the first thing he said was he liked the picture on the wall, a bunch of little handprints in neon colors. I went to read the card under the frame—a gift from the local elementary school, "Hands of the Future," then I misread monoprint as "moonprint." My father flirted with an elderly nurse when she came to take his temp. He made a joke that it was nice to have some time away from the wife, which I know was the one thing bothering him the most. He said, *You're such an animal* because the nurse's smock was the modern kind that had giraffes and turtles on it, the kind my sister wore when she worked in a pediatrician's office.

It turns out that the nurse and my dad went to the same elementary school and they chatted in their childhood French. She couldn't believe the details of the accident—she kept covering her mouth and nodding. She touched the top of her head, when my father told her about my mother. After she left, my father told me his diary was in his top drawer and that I could read if I wanted to when I got home. I had no idea my father kept a diary. I thought maybe he was dreaming, since soon after he fell asleep, his breathing slowing into a purr. I snuck out of the room, trying not to wake him.

I drove home to my mother who asked me over and over again how I thought he was doing. Her friend said she'd been dozing on and off, and once I assured my mother that my father was asleep, she admitted she was tired too and we got her to bed. I slid open my father's drawer and found the same kind of marble-covered notebook I had in high school, but now, because of my misreading, the black and white cover looked like cloudprints.

I read what my father'd written after his surgery a few years ago—that he felt close to God and hoped that the feeling would last. I knew that my father wanted me to know that he was ready, if this infection meant he was going to die. He'd copied prayers and meditations and phrases to take away the pain, and it touched me to see his writing, the actual way he formed his letters. I followed the dates, weeks at a time when he wrote nothing, when everything must have been status quo. Then a friend from his Walmart coffee group died. His other friend (ninety-two) finally let her younger sister (eighty-eight) shovel the driveway instead—my father's commentary, a crooked smiley face.

I put a Percocet in a paper cup on my mother's nightstand in case she woke up and needed another one. My father's rosary was slung over his side of the headboard. My mother's face looked so small on her pillow, I climbed in and took my father's spot. Outside the big white painkiller lay in the sky's palm, a moonprint.

W

The stitches are a crude purple "W" on my mother's scalp. I am so afraid to clean her wounds, even with my latex gloves and bottle of saline, even with my Neosporin and my sterile swabs. How beautiful my mother was as a bride, her upswept wisps, the long sleeves of her gown ending in a V on each of her hands. How beautiful she was on the Staten Island ferry with her long hair tossed to one side by the wind. I think about her childhood Shirley Temple ringlets and later her long spiral curls that covered her nipples—she wore a grass skirt that my uncle brought home from the war—as her arms waved in a hula dance in 1946, the way millions of girls have danced the hula dance ever since. But now her hair is all gone, her head a labyrinth of pus and scabs. *A hurried rat can't figure out a maze*, someone told me recently. He was talking about creativity and now I am that rat, the stunned one, trying to find my way with my Neosporined swab.

I face the swelling, the blue and pickled bulges. My father turns away when I peel off my mother's dressing, the sterile tape, the big sterile pads, the shredding cotton dotted with blood. He's reliving the accident, I can tell. My sister sinks into the chair, blanched, then gets up to help. I tell my mother to keep her dressing on when she brushes her teeth, afraid she'll glimpse her torn scalp when she raises her head after spitting into the sink. She lifts her neck slowly, like she's wearing a Carmen Miranda headdress. We called her Marge Simpson in the hospital, the first joke, her bandages piled high like a bouffant. She can only brush her teeth with her left hand, her right not strong enough yet.

The new doctor says, *Oh dear,* when my mother takes off her glamorous kerchief and Jackie O sunglasses (my idea) to cover the yellow pools of blood that have replaced her cheeks. The surgeon who stitched up my mother promised that he indeed was a good surgeon—it's just that he had to act fast, before she bled to death, her scar a big sloppy W—for Woonsocket, her hometown, for Warrior Woman, for Wonder and Willingness and Wishing her Well.

Washing My Father's Hair

He can't take a shower because of his IV, the stitches on his hand. His whole body hurts, the kidney-shaped bruises on his side—plum lumps—the stiffness in his arms and legs. He bends his head into the sink, and I test the water's temperature and spray his hair with the same gadget I use to rinse the dishes. His hair darkens from white to gray. I accidentally squirt my shirt. I suds him hard because I know it's the one thing that might feel good. I once was small enough to take a bath in this same kitchen sink, not that I'm the same "I" anymore, our longest living cells lasting only ten years. I remember his wedding ring on the side of the soap dish and the way he wrapped me in a towel. Now his ring is jagged from the accident, not quite a circle anymore. I rinse him out fast when his back starts to cramp. I sit him down and rub his head as dry as I can. The comb makes rows where I used to practice the alphabet on his head.

Healing Pies

After my parents' accident, the pies kept coming: chicken pot pies (sized for one person), blueberry pies, ice cream pies, peach cobblers, lemon meringues, pecan pies, pies that were still warm in their tins, apple pies, another chicken pot pie (a big square one), pies with chocolate pudding inside, rhubarb pies, cherry pies, pies with crisscross slats of crust on top. Pies from the church, pies from my mother's quilting group, pies from the neighbors, pies from the aunts. Pies lined the kitchen counter, pies packed the freezer. Holy pies, pies with painkiller filling, herbal pies, prayer pies, pies that kept vigil, pies brimming with novenas, pies full of secrets that even doctors don't know, magic spell pies, smooth soothing pies overflowing with the music of rainforests, pies made from circles of light, pies with halos.

Urban Legend

My parents were in an escalator accident. A pileup. Fourteen people. My mother lost her hair and almost bled to death. My father's heart went out of whack. They were rushed to an emergency room in Atlantic City. The doctors were having trouble finding enough tetanus for everyone hurt. It sounds like an urban legend, except it really happened.

When I take the plane to New Jersey, it's September 11, 2003. I'm almost the only passenger on Spirit Air. I've packed scarves, lots of scarves, to bring to my mother in the hospital. The scarves are the ones Nick's mother wore before she got Alzheimer's. *What about this one?* Nick says, holding up the black and pink flowers. *Or this one?* He holds up the yellow stripes. The purple and white checks.

I sit next to a businessman who has a bad back, who had originally wanted to drive home in one of the company cars, but his job ran late and he's lost his wedding ring and his wife isn't happy. I tell him about the escalator accident, what I know so far, and I call it a freak accident and it occurs to me for the first time that's what it is.

The escalator accident, the escalating conflict in Iraq, fears escalate, escalating tensions. . . . I see the word escalate everywhere in the newspaper I hold in my lap.

I insist that the hospital let my sister and me see our parents, even though it's past visiting hours. My father says that he is fine, but the nurse points to the heart monitor where there are dangerous dips in the hills. He wants to see his wife two floors above him in a different ward. My mother is in a room with someone else from the same accident, a woman who says she was covered with my mother's blood. My mother makes a dry-cleaning joke then squeezes her morphine drip. My sister and I don't know what to do with ourselves when we leave the hospital at midnight, so we to go to the sinister smoky casino hotel. We get lost in a maze of mirrored hallways trying to find our room. All night long we hear the machines: ring, ping, clink, ka-ching. And an occasional siren.

Speaking of legends:

A few weeks later, taking care of my parents, I pray on the wooden floor inside my childhood bedroom. By now the moon is a bowl of cereal my parents are too weak to eat. I get on my knees, keep my back straight. I don't cheat.

Urban Legend Inquest

My father was a cheese grater
My mother was a stair
I'm a no-nonsense escalator
Less I couldn't care . . .

—EDWIN DENBY

I try to get my parents the best lawyer in New Jersey, but when I call his office the secretary tells me, *I'm sorry, honey. Don't say another word. I know the accident you're talking about, but we're representing the casino.*

> Deposition #1: I was just about to step on the escalator when people started falling like dominoes, well not dominoes exactly since that implies order . . .

> Deposition #2: I don't even like casinos. I took the senior bus trip to Cape May, but we had a one-day excursion to Atlantic City. I thought, "What the heck . . ." It was my eightieth birthday, I was feeling lucky . . .

I, _____, the undersigned, on behalf of myself, my heirs and next of kin, personal representative, agents, insurers, successors and assigns (all hereinafter "Releasers") hereby FOREVER RELEASE, DISCHARGE AND COVENANT NOT TO SUE . . .

> Deposition #3: Anyone who could still walk was taken to see the doctor on the casino premises. He stitched us up, he bandaged our cuts. We weren't thinking when we signed the waiver. My glasses had fallen off in the accident so I couldn't even read the small print. My leg was infected by the time I got home, but I was on my own . . .

I acknowledge that I have had sufficient opportunity to review the provisions of this document and understand its purpose, meaning, and intent . . .
(Patient's Signature)_____(Date)_____

> Deposition #4: When I fell, my earring got caught. My lobe split open, a parting curtain . . .

> Deposition #5: When I finally pulled out my hand, it looked as though my fingers had been bitten off by a shark . . .

I steal the New Jersey phone book from the hotel. I call the lawyers who practice casino law. I find someone who is optimistic about my parents' case.

> Deposition #6: My skirt was caught. When the men pulled me up, it was shredded, almost gone. All that was left was the waistband and a few jagged strips of cloth . . .

Individuals who are injured by an escalator that fails to function properly may seek compensation for the injuries they sustained. Escalators in all buildings are required to be kept in safe working order in accordance with local, state, and federal building codes. If you were caught by an escalator, or suffered other escalator injuries, you may have a valid claim for an escalator accident lawsuit.

> Deposition #7: I don't know how it happened, but I was flung from the top. My hair (a short perm) was caught in the moving steps—bump bump bump—against my back. Someone pulled the bodies off of me one by one, and I could finally breathe. Then a man lifted me, too, as though I were as light as a dust mote. He sat me against the wall. Someone else dropped my purse into my lap. My husband found me and curled around me like a cashew so I could lean into him . . .

The accident didn't make the newspaper, any TV shows. The surveillance tape from the camera at the top of the escalator disappeared.

> Deposition #8: I was sandwiched between people for a while, but when I got up I started looking for my wife. I saw her sitting on the floor. I tried to walk toward her, her bloody face, but then I got dizzy and started to crawl. My wife's eyes were as blank as tokens. I remember the yellow chips, polka dots on the carpet. They must have belonged to the other people on the escalator. Coupons for complimentary lunches. A few passers-by picked up the free money, quarters streaked with blood darkening their days . . .

In 1978, New Jersey became the second state to legalize gambling in an attempt to revitalize the rundown resort area. Casinos were expected to be a way for Atlantic City to become a popular tourist destination.

Deposition #9: Workers shielded those most hurt from the stares of tourists out for a drink and a game of slots. Then the ambulance workers came with their stretchers . . .

Legal casino gambling is expected to be the salvation of the moribund resort and possibly the source of a bonanza for the Mob. (*Time*, May 16, 1977)

Deposition #10: My foot got caught in the gap between the steps and the side. I could see the blood coming through my espadrille . . .

The number of elevators exceeds escalators by a factor of twenty, yet there are almost the same number of accidents for both machines. This means that you are almost twenty times more likely to have an accident on an escalator compared to an elevator. (www.verticalanalysis.com)

Deposition #11: It felt like I was being sucked through a straw . . .

New Jersey law requires that slot machines, one-armed bandits, are required to be programmed for a minimum payout of 83 percent.

Deposition #12: I have teeth marks on my side, the exact pattern of the escalator . . .

But the casino won't pay out since they are going bankrupt, changing their name. The escalator company says the casino is at fault since they didn't properly maintain it. . . . The slot machines keep whirring. Bars, dollar signs, the number 7.

Deposition #13: I was lucky. When I felt the escalator buckle, I had just gotten on so I jumped off, backward. But I saw what the escalator did to my handbag. It devoured the strap, then chewed right through the zipper. My wallet, my lipstick, my glasses, my tissue pack tumbled out. I kept thinking that the escalator would jam or turn itself off, but no, the steps just kept going.

The slot machine is carefully designed to be aesthetically pleasing. . . . It features lit buttons and what we found to be a somewhat soothing, hypnotizing sound as the reels are spinning. Moreover, the sound that is played when coins are bet is the same as the sound played when coins are won in a payout, which probably helps make a more positive association. (Michael Shanks)

Deposition #14: It was too beautiful a day to spend in a casino, so I told my friend Sally to go on in and I headed toward the boardwalk to get an ice cream cone.

My parents' case never goes to trial. When they get their settlement, they throw away their bloody clothes and shred a prospectus for a preconstruction seaside condo. My sister takes the pictures of my mother, her injuries, out of the safe and burns them in the fireplace.

Photo Op

We had to take pictures of you for the lawyer. The scar, the zigzagged mess of it, so much blood matted in the few tufts of hair that you had left. The doctor on that first day called you Lucille Ball, but now the blood was stiff and black, not red, and I couldn't tell the hair from the stitches from the blood from the bruises. We took you into the hospital shower, and I stood on the toilet so that I'd be above you, so you wouldn't have to bend to show me your head. I put on the flash and snapped the red-black map of your scalp. Then you let me take pictures of your back—your whole right side, your shoulder to your knee, one big bruise, black like a banana right before you throw it out. There were soft pockets of blood above your waist and the waistband of your pants hurt, so we kept you halfway unzipped. We dressed you in dad's button-down shirt since we dared not put one of your own pullovers over your tender head.

You wanted to wash up, but we were afraid of the showerhead, that it would be too strong for your scalp. The nurse gave us a white giant Styrofoam cup and I squirted your hairline with antibacterial soap and rinsed out the blood that swirled brown in the drain. That was good, you said, since it was old blood stuck to your head coming out. We rinsed until you were too tired to stand anymore. The towel I dabbed your hairline with was brown and the collar of dad's shirt was brown by the time we got home, the damp hair at your hairline dripping onto your neck. I bought you a pink sweater (forty-eight dollars at the gift shop, you'd be mad if you knew I paid that much) that buttoned down the front and I kept thinking I can never live through this, but I was living through it, and buttoning up my mother, trying not to hurt her arm and shoulder. Modest as ever, you telling us you were sorry we had to see you like this. I thought you were talking about your bruises, but no you were talking about your breasts and obsessed about not being able to wear your bra home because the strap would dig into your battered shoulder.

We got you and dad into the limousine where you whimpered that every bump hurt. We tried to make it fun by eating the free potato chips and drinking the Diet Coke, but it wasn't fun. Dad was sitting stiffly in the back, everything hurting him, and you kept trying to move your arm, hold onto the handle above the window, prop yourself up different ways with pillows. Then we asked the driver to pull into the rest stop (mostly for me, but you needed to go too) and dad stayed in the car rather than even get out and stretch, he was that tired, and you and I took tiny steps to the bathroom, your yellow kerchief making you look like a grand dame who just wants her privacy, and we finally made it in. The toilet seat was so low you couldn't get up yourself and I jiggled the lock and got into your stall and tried to lift you up which would have been easy except that I didn't know where I could grab you to hoist—nowhere it turns out, since everything hurt so much. We just kept rocking, trying, your one strong arm around my shoulder, and you were finally standing. I zipped your pants, again only halfway, and we hobbled back to the limo the casino provided and the driver acted as though we weren't there, the way he must have learned to act when his customers had a lot more fun in the backseat. I sat on the floor then so you could lie down. There were no seatbelts so I spotted you in case you rolled. Dad by now was almost asleep.

By the time we rode into Connecticut, it was dusk and the cars started to put on their headlights. You started to doze too, but then the lights made you flinch, as though you were getting ready for your close-up again.

big tip

Sipping Café con Leche Where the Bombs Fell

Palomares, Spain

The girl who serves us wears her jeans low on her hips,
like our students do back in the States. Forty years ago,
a B-52 bomber crashed into a tanker while refueling, dropping
four hydrogen bombs. Three landed around Palomares and one splashed
into the Mediterranean. Nick and I'd come to look for craters
in the fields, but our search wasn't yielding much,
so we stopped for a break.
The waitress who steams the milk
couldn't have been alive in 1966, but maybe her parents were
living here then, children at the time, celebrating the festival of Saint Anthony,
the town's patron saint. It is said *San Antonio* saved the lives
of many people who would otherwise have been farming
when plutonium clouds blew across the crops. The blasts
broke windows, cracked walls, and threw several people to the ground.
We are hesitant to ask the waitress if she knows anything
about "Broken Arrow" because a few days ago we heard on the radio
that owners of the land still deemed tainted are being asked to sell it
at reduced prices for cleanup, so that nine hectares can eventually be made
into a park. What we've read suggests people in Palomares are upset,
still have their urine tested yearly for plutonium levels.

On January, 17, 1966,
Simo Orts was fishing. *We always used to watch the planes.*
I saw a B-52 and a KC-135. They must have brushed against each other.
Both planes burst. I get this all from transcripts of a documentary
about the Cold War. Antonia Flores said, *I remember all this fire in the air*
and pieces of airplane falling to the ground, all the neighbors running
to the place where the smoke came from. We thought that what had fallen there
was still burning.

We almost postponed driving out to Palomares
because we woke up to the news that North Korea had tested a nuclear bomb.
The whole expedition became a bit more obscene, but then we decided
a bit more important as well. Kim Jong Il was no longer the funny man
with the bouffant and platforms, the spoiled leader who ate lobsters
with silver chopsticks. What did we know about North Korea?
Nick said they have their own form of Coca-Cola, "Ko-ko-a"

and that the people are told that Kim was born on Korea's highest mountain,
under a double rainbow. I remembered reading about the red stars
on their license plates.

The last time we were here, in 1995,
Nick and I zoomed by these fields where the three bombs fell, the Beatles
on the rental car's CD player: *I don't care too much for money,*
money can't buy me love. We swam in the Mediterranean, in the waters
where the fourth bomb plummeted. We knew nothing of the incident.
There wasn't much here then—just a scruffy naturalist beach
with a comical sign, a drawing of swimming trunks with a circle around it
and a red line through it. As we peeled off our bathing suits, we felt a little
like John Lennon and Yoko Ono, who posed nude for their first
collaborative album, *Two Virgins,* which was distributed wrapped
in a brown paper covering, sometimes confiscated as pornography. We loved
that Lennon described Yoko and himself as "two slightly overweight,
flabby junkies." It is rumored that he often walked around naked
at the Dakota. And on his last day on earth, Annie Leibovitz photographed him,
nude again, for the most famous cover of *Rolling Stone,* in a pose that looks
as though he is a koala clinging to Yoko, a tree.

In 1995, there was no
chiringuito to get coffee or a snack, none of the 2,000 apartments
that have sprung up—a naturalist community that, according to its advertising,
also welcomes "textiles," which we assume are people who wear clothes.
There are cranes in the sky, cement trucks, piles of bricks,
construction everywhere. There's even a sparkly oversized *supermercado*
called Consum where Nick buys microwavable paella and cartons
of Don Simon gazpacho.

Now our waitress is singing along to her iPod.
We wonder if she is listening to the Beatles, or if anyone her age still listens
to them. John Lennon was staying down the road, in Santa Isabel,
in 1966, when students first wore their jeans low on their hips.
He wrote "Strawberry Fields" while in Spain. He arrived
in October, ten months after the bombs fell. Did he know about them?
Did he make a similar pilgrimage to Palomares? He was still married
to Cynthia then, shooting *How I Won the War.* He would meet Yoko
in November, when he returned to London, wearing for the first time
what became his signature round granny eyeglasses.

Simo Orts: *I saw it*

very clearly. A bomb fell into the sea, close to me. And then I saw
how much interest the Americans showed. The whole Sixth Fleet came.
There were 5,000 soldiers living in tents—generals, colonels, so many
important people from North America. Antonia Flores: *They started*
doing medical checkups here in the town with a Geiger counter.
Some people had to throw away their clothes because they were contaminated.
The houses were washed down with detergent or water.
At no stage did the Americans tell us anything. People were scared,
because no one knew what was happening; all you knew was
that you were forbidden to eat things, that you couldn't go out onto the street,
you couldn't touch anything.

      Vera Playa, the naturalist zone, is believed to be
where Hannibal's elephants landed in Roman times. Spain has been host
to the largest living animals, the largest bombs. In Palomares,
on January 17, 1966, a thirty-knot wind was blowing from the west.
One plutonium-bearing dust cloud traveled across irrigated fields
and the northern edge of the village. Another floated away from the village
but across prime areas used for growing beans and alfalfa.
The last tomato crop of the season, just ready for harvest,
had to be destroyed.

     In *How I Won the War,* Lennon plays Corporal Gripwood,
a fascist fighting against fascism. All the soldiers who die in the film
continue to accompany their units. The director, Richard Lester, shot the film
in black and white, but tinted the uniforms of the dead soldiers in different colors.
The lab that made the release print, assuming the tinting was a mistake,
graded it back to black and white. So no one has ever seen the film
as it was intended.

     Kim Jong Il apparently has several spitting-image doubles
who make public appearances for him. The stand-ins are schooled in the leader's
mannerisms and take voice lessons to sound like him. They've had plastic surgery
so their faces match Kim's. They are used as decoys to foil assassins. The situation
makes for an interesting screenplay. In 1978, the real Kim Jong Il kidnapped
his favorite South Korean director and his girlfriend.

           Before stopping
for coffee, Nick and I drove the perimeter of the town—farmers still bent
in sprouts, the craters perhaps now all filled in. We couldn't find anything—
a plaque or a monument to the crash—only a new *hamburguesa.* Billboards
for more townhouse developments, some newer ranches and bungalows

with swing sets and round above-ground pools.

All four crew members
in the ignited KC-135 tanker were killed. Four of the seven in the B-52
were able to parachute to safety. Volatile materials in two of the bombs
that fell to earth exploded upon impact, forming the holes we thought
we would find. The third landed in a dry riverbed in one piece.
It took almost four months, until April 7, to find the last bomb, damaged but intact,
in the ocean.

In the movie *Men of Honor,* Cuba Gooding Jr. plays Carl Brashear
who, diving from the salvage ship USS *Hoist,* becomes a hero for recovering
the bomb from the bottom of the Mediterranean. Brashear was hurt much worse
than is portrayed in the film. He almost died from loss of blood and gangrene.
His leg was amputated in two operations because of the infection. In real life,
a Spanish fisherman, who witnessed the bomb plunge, led Brashear
and others to the site. I wonder if Kim Jong Il has seen *Men of Honor,*
as he is reported to have 20,000 Hollywood movies in his collection.
Someone told me the dictator said he'd forgo his nuclear ambitions
for just one night with Angelina Jolie. At first I believed it, but soon I found out
that the story was from *Humor Gazette.*
I was mixing up Angelina
with Cicciolina, Jeff Koons's porn star wife who got herself elected
to the Italian Parliament. In 1990, trying to stop the Gulf War, she offered
to have sex with Saddam Hussein, hoping to achieve peace
in the Middle East. She made the same offer in 2002 in exchange
for letting in inspectors to look for WMDs. Cicciolina even offered herself
to Osama bin Laden in return for the end of his tyranny. She was fifty-five by then,
but still up for the job.

After the bombs dropped in Palomares,
a massive clean-up operation was mounted by American authorities.
Some 1,400 tons of radioactive Spanish soil were taken to South Carolina
for disposal. As part of its compensation, the U.S. settled
with 500 Palomares residents whose health was adversely affected.
The United States also built a desalination plant at Vera Playa.
A British couple at the next table tells us they've cancelled their trip
to Pennsylvania Dutch Country because of the schoolhouse shooting.
How could that happen? they ask us. They are polite, truly perplexed. Pensioners,
living part-
time in Palomares, they know about "Broken Arrow" and explain

that in 1966, some of the personnel fell in love with Andalusia's weather
and decided to stay on. A few Americans—though the Brits don't know
their names—still live in the area, retired now. At the time the plant was built,
there was little local development, so it was never put to use. But some
of these roads, they say, were actually paved by the U.S.

                                                      The waitress arrives
with our *la cuenta* and a smile. *You're from the states, si?*

                                                             This is our chance.
The young woman speaks English, but I can't find the right way to ask her
my questions. I try small talk, hoping to build up to a suitable moment.
She is polite—she did indeed grow up here. She is a student on her way
to university next year. Then her cell phone rings and she excuses herself,
giggling all the way to the counter of *tapas,* as Nick empties
his pockets of coins. He leaves a big tip.

                                                  In 1966, the Spanish feared
that their beloved Mediterranean was contaminated. So American Ambassador
Biddel Duke went swimming for the cameras. A "textile," he wore trunks
with red, white, and blue stripes. An interviewer asked,
Ambassador, do you detect any radioactivity in the water?
And Duke answered, *If this is radioactivity, I love it.*

Anagram America

You may say America is **a crime, a**
lens cap locked onto its own **camera. I**
may agree but sidetrack you with our crazy cartoon products by **Acme, IRA**
accounts, our Hollywood films, a stay at a n**ice Rama-**
da Inn. And what about our generous tax refund system? I **race aim-**
lessly through the stuffed aisles of Dollar-**Rama. Ice**
cube trays and pink sponges and a digital **camera. I**
buy them all! Now that's America. In Skate-a-**Rama, ice**
skaters figure-eight even in summer. **I race, Ma-**
donna on the speakers, my laces tight. Sure, the arms **race (aim-**
ing to make peace through the threat of violence) is **a crime, a-**
bout-face logic, to boot. But what politician can say so on **camera? I**
watched *The Crying Game,* but not to better understand the **IRA.** *Came-*
lot, Man of La Mancha. How I love movies! "**Mira!**" **Came-**
o appearances—I'm the first to spot them. A director, a writ**er. A cami-**
sole and lipstick distract you, but not me. Inside my watch is a tiny spy **camera. I**
never miss a clue. I'm an undercover agent, ma'**am. I care**
about civil liberties, though, and still believe in the ACLU—**a crime, a**
naive throwback, I'm told. America tends to m**aim, care-**
ful not to kill at first. We're all for democracy or so we cl**aim, care-**
less with our rhetoric. The Korean became Vietnamese be**came Ira-**
qi. A corporate crime is a war crime is **a crime, a**
passionate one at that. But first play n**ice. Rama-**
dan starts tomorrow. We don't want to cause any disg**race, ami-**
gos. (We're off to Abu Graib, so let's recharge that **camera.) I**
am all for the way the "eye" becomes the "I," **camera-**
ready, happy to shoot and be shot, the web **cam. I race**
to turn on CNN, but there is nothing about the war. Instead, Shak**ira came**
on shaking her hips in Spanish. Her **mica ear-**
rings shone. Dancing in a language other than English is **a crime, a**
topic, said the senator, for the next political **race, aim-**
ing for the wallflower vote. Oh news **camera, I**
know a commercial when I see it. Medi**care, I am**
on my way. Welcome to **America**
where the letters can be twisted into almost anything, even **Ma, I care.**

Weapons Inspectors' Checklist

written August 4, 2002 (then translated from English to Ilocano and Ilocano to Tagalog by Luisa A. Igloria; from Tagalog to Spanish by Nick Carbó; from Spanish to Italian by Nina Romano; from Italian to French by Andrée Conrad; from French to German by Susanne Nielsen; and from German back to English—these lines shown in italics—by Astrid Parish)

Do they have nerve gas?

Do they have nerve gas?

Do they have tear gas?

Do they have tear gas?

Do they have gas?

Do they have gas?

Gas-powered stoves?

Can they change the settings on the tank?

Gas grills?

Do they have gas for the grill?

Do they pump their own gas?

Is the gas in this forsaken land rationed?

Do gases swirl in curlicues above their deplorable country?

Do they live under free skies beneath small disappearing combustible clouds?

Is their sky dotted with small flammable clouds?

Do their clouds explode?

Do they have smallpox?

Do they have measles?

Do they have pock marks?

Are their faces covered with acne spots?

Do they have chicken pox?

Do they have chicken pox?

Do they have chicken farms?

Do they have enclosed yards?

Do they have chicken farmers?

Do they have coq au vin?

Do those farmers also raise potbellied pigs?

Do the farmers look for first quality pork bellied pigs?

Do they have potbellied stoves?

Are their pigs fatty?

Do they have potholes?

Or are their fatty pigs simply overfed?

Do they have proximity to those potholes?

Are they neighbors?

Do they have pots?

Do they have pots?

Do they cook in those pots?

Do they cook in these pots?

And if so, what kinds of strange meals do they make?

When it's "the fall," what sorts of food do they cook?

Do they make anthrax?

Do they make anthrax?

Do they know how to disperse anthrax?

Do they know how to distribute anthrax?

Do they sell anthrax to terrorists?

Is it possible that they sell anthrax to terrorists?

Do they have a T. J. Maxx?

Do they know a man called T. J. Maxx?

Do they have a cineplex?

Do they have a cineplex?

What do they show in those cineplexes?

What plays at their local cineplex?

Do they have showbiz?

Do they have show business?

Do they have monkey biz?

Do they have monkey business?

Do they have memories of the Byzantine Empire?

How can they possibly remember the Byzantine Empire?

Do they have *The Empire Strikes Back* on DVD?

Are they able to have strong enough shoulders to handle a strike in the DVD plant?

Do they have backbone?

Do they have the main element?

Do they wave skull-and-bone flags?

Do they steal banners from pirates?

Are they numskulls?

Are they dumb?

Are we numskulls?

Are we dumb?

Are we numb by now to baseball strikes?

Do they compare the stupid outcomes of all the baseball strikes then laugh?

Do they have baseball?

Do they have baseball?

Do they have balls?

Do they have balls?

Do they have disco balls?

Do they have bowling leagues?

Do they have ball-and-chain prisons?

Do they have prisons in which iron balls swing on chains?

Do they have chain link fences?

Do they wear identification necklaces?

Do they remember Art Linkletter?

Do they remember Art Linkletter?

Do they have letter bombs?

Do they have bombs made out of paper?

Do they have nuclear bombs?

Do they have nuclear bombs?

Do they have dirty bombs?

Do they have dirty bombs?

Do they have dirty magazines?

Do they have magazines that men enjoy?

Do they have children with dirty faces?

Do they see children whose faces are covered with dirt?

Do they have well-behaved children?

Do they have well-raised children?

Do they have children disguised as soldiers?

Do they disguise their small children as soldiers?

Do they have soldiers disguised as children?

Do soldiers like to dress up as children?

Are their children products of their environment?

Where do all these products manufactured for children come from?

Do they create an environment of hate?

Do they have a tendency toward hatred?

Do their children hate going to school as much as ours?

Would they like their children to be raised as well as ours are?

Do their children hate us?

Do they hate their own children?

Do their children hate the notion of biological warfare?

Are their children against chemical-biological warfare?

Do they dread their biology tests?

Do they tremble with fear before chemical-biological weapons inspectors?

Do mothers there talk about their biological clocks?

Do their mothers talk to them about biology or clocks?

Do they have pencil pushers and clock watchers?

Are there specialists or observers of these forever-changing clocks?

Do they have pedal pushers and girl watchers?

Are there filthy men in cars, or peddling bicycles, on the prowl after young girls?

Is there one small girl there who pedals for peace?

Here is a young girl wearing the garland for the fight for freedom.

Is peace even possible, with so many petals of the flower torn off?

Can one hold onto freedom with orange blossoms?

Do they grow vegetables or flowering plants?

Can we cultivate such vegetation and orange blossoms in our factories?

Do they have chemical plants?

Do they have drug factories?

Do they believe in chemicals like Zoloft or Prozac to ward off depression?

Do they believe that substances such as "Zoloft" and "Prozac" actually work against depression?

Are they ever depressed?

Are these people disadvantaged?

Is their economy depressed?

Are these people economically disadvantaged?

Is their economy in the doldrums?

Do they live in the neighborhood?

Are their clothes dull?

Does their very substance reassure them?

Are their comics dull?

Sadly, their comedians are without strength.

Does anyone there even read the comics?

Does anyone in this land bother to read the comic strips?

Do they have strip malls?

Do they have design shops?

Do they have strip clubs and sex shops?

Do they have discos, cabarets, sex shops, and more?

Does anyone there ever use sex as a weapon?

Are there people in this land whose sexual activity can create bombs?

Do they have weapons of mass destruction?

Where are your weapons of wholesale destruction? Please tell us.

Are the masses nervous?

Are the masses fearful?

Do they have the nerve?

If you have the rash audacity, just do it.

Acknowledgments

Grateful acknowledgment is made to the editors and staff members of the magazines and antholgies in which poems from *Ka-ching!* first appeared:

Bat City Review ("Photo Op"); *Cake* ("Hurricane Katrina"); *Cincinnati Review* ("Dinner Party Horror"); *Coconut* ("$200,000," "$400,000," "$500,000," "Apple," and "Stupid Vanilla"); *Columbia Poetry Review* ("'Please Don't Sit Like a Frog, Sit Like a Queen'"); *Court Green* ("$900,000"); *5 a.m.* ("The Da Vinci Poke"); *Florida Review* ("Spoon"); *Gargoyle* ("Healing Pies" and "My Mother's Hair"); *Gulf Coast* ("A Dog and a Boy" and "Moonprint"); *Home Planet News* ("Cinderella's Ghost Slipper"); *Indiana Review* ("$600,000"); *International Literary Quarterly* ("Sipping Café con Leche Where the Bombs Fell"); *Margie* ("$300,000"); *McSweeney's* ("Delta Flight 659" as "On Delta Flight 659 with Sean Penn" and "I Dreamed This Sestina Wearing My Maidenform Bra"); *Michigan Quarterly Review* ("Repeat"); *Mudlark* ("$700,000," "$800,000," and "$1,000,000"); *Natural Bridge* ("Perimenopause"); *North American Review* ("Weapons Inspectors' Checklist"); *Ontario Review* ("No Home-Wrecker"); *Paragraph* ("Girl Talk"); *Prairie Schooner* ("Anagram America" and "Urban Legend"); *Schuylkill Valley Journal of the Arts* ("Washing My Father's Hair"); *Sentence* ("The Language Police" and "W"); *Shade* ("Casino"); *Smartish Pace* ("eBay sonnets"); *Specs* ("Urban Legend Inquest"); *Sub-lit* ("What Women Know"); *Sycamore Review* ("Basically"); *Toaster Mag* ("$100,000"); *Triquarterly* ("Lucky Me").

"Basically," "Casino," "A Dog and a Boy," "Dinner Party Horror," "Lucky Me," "No Home-Wrecker," "'Please Don't Sit Like a Frog, Sit Like a Queen,'" "Perimenopause," "Urban Legend," "W," "Washing My Father's Hair," and "Weapons Inspectors' Checklist" also appear in a bilingual edition of my work, *Afortunada de mi* (Madrid: Bartleby Editores, 2008).

"Weapons Inspectors' Checklist" was reprinted in *Gulfstreaming* (2003). "Lucky Me" was reprinted in *E-X-C-H-A-N-G-E-V-A-L-U-E-S: The Second XV Interviews* (2007). "The Language Police" was reprinted in *The Best American Poetry 2007.* "'Please Don't Sit Like a Frog, Sit Like a Queen'" was reprinted in *The Best American Poetry 2006.* "I Dreamed I Wrote This Sestina Wearing My Maidenform Bra" was reprinted in *The Mind's Eye: A Guide to Writing Poetry* (2008). "Casino" and "My Mother's Hair" were reprinted in *Brevity and Echo* (2006).

"Dinner Party Horror" is for Mitch Corber. "eBay sonnets" is for John D. Freyer. "What Women Know" is for Tony Hoagland and Stephen Dunn.

With many thanks to Stephanie Strickland, who helped shape this manuscript and first suggested the title; to Nick Carbó and Tom Fink, who guided me in rethinking individual poems; and to Florida International University, Virginia Center for the Creative Arts, Civitella, Moulin Nef, and The Corporation of Yaddo, all of which provided support. And with tremendous gratitude to Ed Ochester and all the kind and creative people at University of Pittsburgh Press.